Sometime Samaritans

Fast, Free, and Funny Ways to Do Good
(Even If You're Lazy, Cheap, and Selfish)

Diane L. Pierson

For information, please email Diane Pierson at
sometimesamaritans@gmail.com

eBook ISBN: 979-8-9886601-2-5

Print Book ISBN: 979-8-9886601-4-9

To Tom
Thank you for making my world a better place every day.

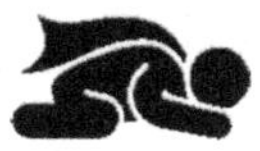

Table of Contents

Introduction

My Life on Good Intentions Highway

I know a lot of good Samaritans. They make the world a better place in ways that require self-sacrifice, financial investment or major time commitments - sometimes all three. They volunteer, they donate, they foster, they rescue. I've always admired my generous friends even though I told myself that I, personally, just couldn't make the world a better place. Not right now, anyway. I was too busy. I hadn't found the right cause. I wasn't financially solvent enough to give enough to make an impact.

What I realized as I got older? None of that is true. I wasn't making the world a better place because I am, in fact, lazy, cheap and selfish. I'm too lazy to be out all day busting hump in the hot sun cleaning up a local park. I'm too cheap to donate money to even the very best of causes. But selfishly, I feel like it's totally unfair that there isn't some way *I* can be a nice person, too. Just without all the hassle. I'm not proud of it, but I'm too lazy to change.

For years I've asked myself: isn't there some way to make the world a better place without it costing me anything, or taking too much time, or, well, inconveniencing me at all? Is there a way to be a *Sometime Samaritan*?

Becoming a Sometime Samaritan

Turns out - there is. Eureka! There are actually *tons* of ways to make the world a better place that take very little time, expend hardly any calories and cost absolutely nothing. Some of these even *save* you time and energy while still doing something positive for humanity. How great is that?

Once I started thinking of them, I started doing them. Well - not much doing, really. I held a few doors open. I complimented speedy checkout clerks. I stopped running red lights. Becoming a Sometime Samaritan was super-easy. Even better, the reaction from the people I barely, lazily helped made it clear that I was making the world a better place. So, I kept doing - not much. And I kept looking for new ideas - and found a bunch.

In fact, there are so many, I decided to make a list of every fast, free, and funny suggestion I could think of for lazy, cheap and selfish people to make the world a better place. To become Sometime Samaritans. That list turned into this book.

How to Change the World by Doing Almost Nothing

Every suggestion in this book will help you make the world a better place by doing almost nothing. To make sure this do-gooderism wouldn't cramp your lazy, selfish style, I set a few strict rules for any suggestion I considered including. As a result, *every idea in the book* meets the following Sometime Samaritan criteria:

It Takes Two Minutes or Less to Complete

Being a well-intentioned but selfish, lazy person usually means we *want* to do good things, but we don't want to do them for more than a few minutes at a time.

No judgment. *I'm* lazy, but not everyone is. For all I know, *you're* working two jobs and raising kids and going to school. You aren't lazy, just *busy*. But whatever the root cause of the inertia, our version of changing the world just can't take too long. So, the first criterion for these world-changing suggestions is that they take almost no time to complete.

Not one single suggestion in the book took me more than 120 seconds to complete - I timed them. Some of these world-changers will even *save* you time. How's *that* for a lazy win-win!

Volunteering for the Saturday-morning park cleanup? Nope. Providing after-school tutoring? Huh-uh. But holding a door open for the person behind me when I'm already walking through it myself? Yeah - I can do that. And so can you.

It Requires Almost No Effort

Whether you're lazy or busy, you're probably pretty tired at the end of your day. I get wiped out binge-watching Netflix, so I understand. There's no way I'm shoveling the neighbor's sidewalk or knitting slippers for a shut-in.

Therefore, these suggestions are designed for the truly lazy. For those who want to change the world but - almost literally - don't want to lift a finger to do it. To meet these criteria, only suggestions that use 10 calories or fewer are included.

I even used some of my precious energy to create a Selfish, Lazy and Cheap - ***SLAC-er*** for short - Activity Scale. The scale is based on time and effort, and I've classified every suggestion into one of three SLAC-er activity levels:

Levels on the "SLAC-er Activity Scale"

Activity Level 1: Negative Effort. Time and / or Effort are Saved.

These suggestions are for the superlatively lazy among us. A suggestion with an Activity Level of 1 actually *saves* you time or *reduces* caloric burn compared to the most typical alternative. This type of world-improving activity is usually one where you *don't* do something, instead of proactively performing an activity. Think: don't honk your horn in traffic. That's right, you can make the world a better place and do *less than nothing*. You're welcome.

Activity Level 2: Almost No Effort. Between 0-30 Seconds and / or 0-5 Calories.

If you're even one baby step more active than the threshold above, there are many more ways you can make the world a better place. While some effort is necessary in Activity Level 2, these suggestions take almost no time or caloric effort. Usually, because they substitute one activity for another or are part of something you're already doing. Saying "Nice job!" to a co-worker who made a huge sale, for example. I mean, c'mon - you're breathing out anyway, just put some words in the breath. Seems like a pretty good deal for less than one calorie!

Activity Level 3: Minimal Effort. Between 30-120 Seconds and/or 6-10 Calories.

For those of you who are *just barely* lazy; if you're willing to wipe a counter, pet a puppy or walk an extra 100 feet (round trip, of course) to change the world, these suggestions are for you.

You'll find plenty of suggestions for each activity level - choose what works for you. Oh, and I estimated caloric expenditures via the highly expedient method of asking AI. So they may be a bit crackpot, but they're close enough for Sometime Samaritans. As you skim through the suggestions, you'll see that I've probably *overestimated* the calories burned to do most of them. That was on purpose. After all, we don't want you inadvertently overdoing it when doing good.

It Requires No Skills

We're not talking Doctors Without Borders here. My third criterion was that you need no special talent to make the world better. As a result, *none* of these suggestions require you to learn a new skill, pay for special training, or even read instructions. You don't have to be particularly smart, particularly skilled or even particularly coordinated. Which means you don't have to wait to change the world until you muster up enough energy to learn how. All of these suggestions can be completed with whatever skills are currently keeping you alive and in ramen noodles.

It Demands No Emotional Investment

You know who you are: the concerned introvert. The distant do-gooder. You want to make the world a better place even though you're not really interested in being too engaged with the people in it. Worry not - you're one of us. The suggestions in this book don't require you to join a group, adhere to a religion or believe in the tenets of any cause. You don't have to pretend to like anybody. For many of these ideas, you don't even have to interact with another human. There are a few recommendations that do, admittedly, require you to be nice, or at least speak, to another person, but you can always skip those.

It Costs You Nothing

Maybe you would give money to charity, but don't have any money to spare. Or not - no judgment. The good news is, there are so many ways to make the world a better place without spending a dime that, even if I wasn't dealing with fellow cheapskates, I might have made this a criteria. My ideas for changing the world won't get your name on the side of a building, but they'll allow you to make the world a better place until you have that bankroll ready.

It's Selfish

Strictly speaking, doing something suggested in this book is unselfish. But Sometime Samaritans are selfish by definition, and we want the world to be a good place for *us,* right? We want other drivers to let us in at a traffic merge. We want strangers to tell us we look fabulous. We want to walk in the woods without wading through piles of discarded socks and soda cans. Most of all - we want credit for making the world a better place by doing as little as possible.

And so - thank you. Your comically small and cheap action will make life better for you, your family and people you'll never meet. It will make the world suck just a little less.

But wait - there's more!

Studies Back Up the Benefits - to YOU

Great news, my selfish SLAC-ers. There's real research showing that the act of doing good for others will make you happier:

- One experiment from the University of Oxford asked participants to engage in small, random acts of kindness for a week, measuring *their own* happiness levels and comparing them with a control group. The result? A big spike in well-being among those who practiced kindness compared with those who did not.

- A study of workers at a Coca Cola plant in Madrid showed that little acts of kindness rippled out through a whole office full of people. After a control group of workers began doing nice things for others in the test, the number of prosocial (a.k.a. nice) acts done by the entire group increased by *ten times* and led to lasting happiness gains.
- Finally, according to a massive recent study positive, happier people are more likely to be successful in life.

This research is so convincing that Yale psychologist Laurie Santos claims the best form of self-care is being kind to others.

I could give you more detail about all these studies, but that really would be a lot of work, so I'm not going to. Check them out if you'd like. Or ask your favorite AI bot. The upshot is, if you lurch off the couch and do even one of these suggestions each week, you'll be promoted at work, get rich, grow more beautiful and reverse the aging process.

Don't Strain Yourself

Nobody expects you to become a martyr to doing good. We're *Sometime* Samaritans, so I recommend doing one or two of these suggestions each week. Feel free to pick and choose what's easiest for you. Don't strain yourself. After that? Well, if you're in the mood, do more. If not - no worries.

If you're in the top ranks of the truly lazy, cheap and selfish, remember: just one action, done one time, gets you credit for positively impacting the world around you. Just. One.

Now: let's get you out there changing the world! One lazy, cheap, and selfish act at a time.

1. Put More Than One Grape in That Plastic Produce Bag

Guess what's *not* a rule? It's not a rule that you have to use a separate plastic bag for each piece of produce you grab at the grocery store. What if you weighed your papayas, got your little sticky-label, and just put them right in with the carrots, kumquats, and turnips you already packed up? Add the new sticky to the existing plastic bag and - done! This costs you less effort than walking over, unspooling, and picking open yet another one of those plastic bags from the giant roll by the zucchini. You're saving the planet, one tropical fruit at a time.

Time Spent: Negative
Calories Expended: Negative
Activity Level: 1

SLAC-er Bonus: Extra karmic points if you put all the little sticky price tags on the same side of the plastic bag, so the checker doesn't have to hunt for each one when you're ready to get home for your nap.

2. Keep a Secret

A core motivation of being lazy, cheap and selfish is to avoid work, expense and irritation. Keeping the secret a friend entrusted to you is one of the best ways to live your best life while also making the world a better place. After all, it's hard enough for people like us to keep friends *without* blabbing their deepest darkest to whoever we're standing next to in the food truck line. Keep your lips zipped and validate that misguided trust for a change.

Time Spent: Negative
Calories Expended: Negative
Activity Level: 1

3. Greet the Greeters

Whether big box store or big-time office building, businesses often have someone at the front of the house welcoming you in. So why treat them like they're offering you Ebola? Just stretch a smile, say hi, and move on with your day. Who knows, establishing some rapport may come in handy when you need help figuring out where those on-sale slippers are hiding.

Time Spent: 5 seconds
Calories Expended: <1
Activity Level: 2

4. Lean Into the Slimy Dan's Experience

Don't Spoil the Group Decision

You already caved to the group, which wants to go to Slimy Dan's Hot Dogs* instead of Simply Sushi. But you still have an opportunity to spoil it by moaning about the food, prices or weenie décor. Don't. The group already knows you didn't want to eat hot dogs; make sure your nice gesture stays nice instead of trapping your friends in your gastronomical version of payback. Believe me, the results of eating at Slimy Dan's will do that for you.

Time Spent: Negative
Calories Expended: Negative
Activity Level: 1

SLAC-er Addendum: *Slimy Dan's Hot Dogs is meant to be fictional - apologies if I'm denigrating a real hot dog establishment. Or anyone named Slimy Dan.

5. Use Your Earbuds or Mute the Sound

This one sits firmly under the heading of Things Nobody Should Have to Tell You - even those of us who are in the lazy, cheap, and selfish hall of fame. Nobody wants to hear your status meeting. Nobody is interested in the sounds your game is making. Nobody wants to revisit *Gangnam Style*. Nobody. Keep your earbuds in *just one time* when you would've blared your Minecraft audio and make the world a more peaceful place. Too cheap to buy headphones? Too lazy to remember them? Then watch those South Korean dance moves on the quiet until you're alone.

Time Spent: 5 seconds
Calories Expended: <1
Activity Level: 2

6. Stop at One Red Light You Would've Run

That traffic light isn't orange. Or pink. Or whatever you say to yourself to justify blowing through it. Who knows how much better everyone's day will be if you just - stop? And, while traffic lights may seem interminable, sitting at an extra light each day takes up almost none of your time. According to the National Association of City Transportation Officials (which is a real thing), traffic lights stay red between 60 and 90 seconds on average. That means you'll spend just 75 seconds cooling your wheels at each red light you stop at. Contrast that with the expense and exertion required for a hospital stay and physical therapy. Throw in court dates, fines, and community service; it's a no-brainer for Sometime Samaritans to wait for the next green.

Time Spent: 75 seconds
Calories Expended: <1
Activity Level: 2

SLAC-er Bonus: Here's another real thing: the *IIHS* reports that running a red light or stop sign is the most common (sober) cause of all urban crashes, with over 100,000 injuries in 2023 alone. Your measly 75 seconds could save someone's life, including yours.

7. Give Away Found Money

There's nothing we cheap, selfish people love more than finding money. Thirty-eight cents picked out of a puddle at a pig farm can make our whole week. But - it's also an opportunity to change the world while spending no money of your own. Whether you put the change in the next school fundraiser jar you see, or - if you've really hit it big - you buy lunch for a stranger, you were just able to do a little good without spending your own money. Nice! Of course, it should go without saying that there was no way for you to get the money back to its *original* owner; remember you get world-points for that, too.

Time Spent: 2 minutes
Calories Expended: 10
Activity Level: 3

8. Leave Nature Where You Find It

Since you've been forced into a nature hike, picking a few wildflowers or enjoying blackberries fresh from the bush is your selfish right. Right? But think it through - you won't *really* put those dirty, wilty flowers in a vase once you've schlepped them all the way home. As a matter of fact, you'll probably throw them out the car window a mile from where you snatched them. It's easier and longer lasting to snap a picture of those posies, with the added benefit of leaving the flowers where they are for others to enjoy. The blackberries? Eat every single one you see. Life is short.

Time Spent: Negative
Calories Expended: Negative
Activity Level: 1

9. Remind Friends of Fond Memories

It's easy to fall into the ongoing argument about which one of you ate that last Tiny Pie back in 2016, but why not make the world a better place and bring up something mutually festive? "Remember that time we went fishing and, yada yada yada, we had bubble gum for dinner?" A shared memory gives you both a happy hit of feels and, who knows? It may even spark a longer conversation you *want* to participate in.

Time Spent: 30 seconds
Calories Expended: 1
Activity Level: 2

SLAC-er Addendum: You ate that last Tiny Pie. Everyone knows it.

10. Give a "+1" in an Online Meeting

Participation counts in business, but you don't have to pull a hamstring, especially in the online meeting. Too lazy to unmute to mumble, "I agree"? Just type "+1" in the Zoom chat when someone else says something smart. You reward the work of others, and get a teeny tiny participation trophy, while doing almost nothing yourself. SLAC-er nirvana!

Time Spent: 3 seconds
Calories Expended: <1
Activity Level: 2

11. Set Out Breakfast Items for Later Risers

I know who I'm dealing with, so remember I'm not asking you to make breakfast for your housemates. I'm asking you to give them a head start making it for themselves. Who knew *that* could be a win? Setting out breakfast basics like a coffee cup, bowl or box of cereal for whoever you live with makes you look like a hero to your groggy roomies. You're already in the kitchen - you might as well bask in the morning glory! Of course, it's highly possible that *you* are the late riser. If so - feel free to set out plates and silverware for lunch.

Time Spent: 30 seconds
Calories Expended: 3
Activity Level: 2

12. Change the World at 30,000 Feet: Put Your Second Carry-On Under the Seat in Front of You

I know - you'd really rather not have to scrunch up further in your already scrunched-up middle seat on the airplane. But to make the flight a better place, put your second carry-on item underneath the seat in front of you. After all, it's actually been the rule to do so on airplanes since, oh...you were *born*. At the very least, hold on to your puffer jacket, fascinator and that giant bag of pineapples until everyone else gets their first bag into the overhead. If you can squeeze your second item in at that point - you have my blessing.

Time Spent: None
Calories Expended: <1
Activity Level: 2

13. Changed Your Mind? Put It Back Where You Found It

No longer going to buy those pickled papayas? Don't dump them in the dog food aisle. Walk whatever it is back to wherever you got it. Even in a massive grocery store like my local HEB, you can return most items to their proper place in under two minutes. Grocery workers everywhere will thank you.

Time Spent: 2 minutes
Calories Expended: 5
Activity Level: 3

SLAC-er Tip: Just can't work up the energy to take that foot powder all the way back to Aisle 5? Hand it to the clerk when you check out. It's better than stashing it in the ice cream freezer.

14. Wait, Watt?

Turn Your Thermostat Down One Degree

According to the U.S. Department of Energy, the average American could save between $70-100 on their electricity bill just by turning the heat down *one measly degree*. That means you'd pocket real savings while leaving a few watts for the other humans. Actually, a *lotta* watts. If everyone in the U.S. turned their thermostat down just a single degree, and only in the winter, we'd save enough juice to run your microwave non-stop for *400,000 years*. And if your thermostat has a programmable feature, you can set it once and never lift a finger again. Honestly, that might be the highest-impact world-bettering win you can get for the smallest effort. Watt a deal.

Time Spent: 15 seconds
Calories Expended: 3
Activity Level: 2

15. Respectfully Making the World a Better Place

Retire "With All Due Respect"

Non-spoiler spoiler alert: What you're saying when you say, "With all due respect" is, in fact, "I want to point out that I have zero respect for you before I even get to the *direct* insult." Skip the effort it takes to verbalize this snarktactular modifier and rephrase it like a grown-up. People might actually listen instead of plotting your professional demise.

Time Spent: Negative
Calories Expended: Negative
Activity Level: 1

16. Reflect on Something You're Grateful For

Getting in the right frame of mind to do miniscule bits of good in the world is valuable in and of itself. So, reflect on something you're grateful for. It doesn't have to be existential; it could be coffee. Or a nap. Or that your favorite hoodie was clean, so you didn't have to sneak it into your roomie's wash basket. Gratitude lifts your mood, which gets you ready to change the world. And hey - you get extra points if you share the thought or thank whoever did that great thing.

Time Spent: 20 seconds
Calories Expended: <1
Activity Level: 2

17. Give Up That Airport Outlet

Airports are such concentrated hubs of misery that anything you can do to make the experience better for others gives you double karmic points. One easy thing for a Sometime Samaritan? Unplug from that rare and valuable electrical outlet when your device is fully charged. After all, even the most selfish device can't hold more than a 100% charge. You are now the hero of Gate C7.

Time Spent: Neutral
Calories Expended: Neutral
Activity Level: 1

18. Spread the Cred at Work

Most great ideas really are fabulous Frankensteins made from bits that came out of everyone's brains. Even if you had the original thought, odds are someone helped, expanded, or implemented it after your initial brainwave. Spread the love by giving them a public shoutout at the next all-hands meeting. Sharing credit is the generous *and* smart thing to do - building loyalty points in addition to karmic credit from the people you just name-dropped.

Time Spent: 20 seconds
Calories Expended: 3
Activity Level: 2

19. Make a Newbie Feel Welcome with Local Info

Notice a new neighbor in the lobby or doing laundry? While it's tempting to avoid a time-sucking series of welcoming pleasantries, it's also an opportunity to make the world a better place without much effort. Share information about local resources like great blanket stores or tasty takeout. Maybe you have an inside tip on the most languid yoga class in the area. Share a little insight, make them feel welcome, and go back to not folding your t-shirts knowing you did a good thing.

Time Spent: 2 minutes
Calories Expended: 5
Activity Level: 3

20. Maybe *They'll* Make It: Pass Along a Recipe

Look - you know and I know that *we're* never going to make that cashew brittle or potato salad from Aunt Lucy's old recipe file. But *someone* might, if they enjoy cooking. Passing along a favorite recipe is a fun and personal way to inspire someone - other than yourself - in the kitchen. This is especially smart if selfish you knows the cashew brittle is truly delish, and that your culinarily-inclined pal will share the bounty.

Time Spent: 2 minutes
Calories Expended: 3
Activity Level: 3

SLAC-er Bonus: This is my brother-in-law Larry's recipe for baked beans. Who knew baked beans could be so good? And the recipe is easy enough for even a SLAC-er to attempt.

Larry's Homemade Baked Beans
1lb bacon, chopped
1cup onion, chopped
1 cup brown sugar
1 cup water

1 can each: red beans, lima beans, butter beans and white beans, drained.
1 can of pre-made pork and beans, do not drain

Instructions: Preheat the oven to 350 degrees. Cook the chopped bacon on the stovetop for 5 minutes on medium heat; add chopped onions and cook until the onions are translucent, about 5 more minutes, and drain. In a Dutch oven, combine bacon, onion, water and brown sugar as well as all the beans. Cover and cook at 350 degrees for 90 minutes. Then eat. Sharing optional.

21. Send a Thank-You to a Coworker

Some work cultures frown on thanking people who are just doing their job. But it's a SLAC-er opportunity. If Emma from sales answered your contract question? Eduardo from HR helped you fill out an insurance form? Type five words, "Thanks, that really helped today." Hit send. It's professional, thoughtful, and will reinforce whatever good behavior made you need to thank them in the first place.

Time Spent: 15 seconds
Calories Expended: <1
Activity Level: 2

22. Use Old Printed Materials as Scrap Paper

Most of us don't print much anymore, but some of our selfish selves are still making the least of whatever paper we *do* use for printing. Just can't make yourself print on both sides of the paper? Then at least use that pristine *other* side as scrap paper. It requires no effort to stuff these half-used sheets into a corner, periodically staple them together into a "pad" of paper, and use that instead of yet another fresh-killed tree for your packing list and superhero doodles.

Time Spent: 1 minute
Calories Expended: 3
Activity Level: 2

23. Obey the Rules of the Aisle, Sidewalk, and Bike Path

Have you ever done the Aisle 5 Tango with an oncoming shopper because you're walking *up* and they're walking *down* the same side of the passage? Help make movement more enjoyable for all concerned by minding the rules of the "road" even when you're pushing a cart at Target or walking into that dentist appointment. In the U.S., this means staying on the *right* side of an aisle, hallway or path in any two-way flow of traffic. Pass on the left only when that lane is clear and remember that oncoming traffic has the right of way. I mean, c'mon - it's not like you *want* to touch those people you keep bumping into.

Time Spent: Neutral
Calories Expended: Neutral
Activity Level: 1

24. Wipe Out the Sink When You're Done

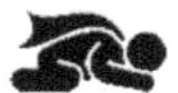

Even someone bound to you in sickness and in health didn't say, "I do" to a sink full of toothpaste globs and body hair, much less those semi-strangers you share the rent with. A clean(ish) sink starts everyone's day off right. And you know what a difference a little effort would make, don't you? The picture in your head of what your sink looks like *right now* should be enough to make you grab a tissue, towel or hazmat suit and do a quick wipe-out.

Time Spent: 1 minute
Calories Expended: 3
Activity Level: 2

25. Weigh and Tag Your Produce

You know how much time and effort it takes to weigh those two nectarines, grab your little sticky price tag, put it on a plastic bag and make your cashier's life a little easier? You do now:

Time Spent: 1 minute
Calories Expended: 2
Activity Level: 3

26. Remove Trash from Your Car

Your car is not a mobile dumpster - dump that trash before it multiplies to the point of affecting your social life. While this suggestion is intended to make the world better for your passengers, it gets a little selfish plus because you benefit from it too. The *other* great news about this suggestion is that you can do it on your way to something fun. There are trash cans everywhere - who knew?

Time Spent: 30 seconds
Calories Expended: 3
Activity Level: 2

27. Get Something Off a High (or Low) Shelf for Someone

Grocery stores offer some amazing opportunities to do good by doing almost nothing. This is one of my faves: are you freakishly tall (like me) or a little on the stumpy side? Either one makes you a valuable helper in reaching the unreachable product, be it on the tip-py-top shelf or the back of the bottom. Put your stature superpower to good use and help a struggling fellow shopper snag that elusive bag of Funyuns.

Time Spent: 20 seconds
Calories Expended: 3
Activity Level: 2

28. It's Been a Minute - Send a Text

If you really do like these people you say you're friends with, you *have* to interact with them occasionally no matter how lazy and selfish you are. A quick, "I've been thinking about you - hope you're well" text, with maybe a puppy or flower emoji thrown in for good measure, keeps you in the marginally-thoughtful-friend category.

Time Spent: 20 seconds
Calories Expended: 1
Activity Level: 2

29. Add It to the List

Emptied the ketchup bottle? Finished that carton of Krimpets? Took the last one of whatever? Put it on the grocery list so those people you live with don't experience condiment withdrawal. Extra Sometime Samaritan SLAC-er points if you actually do this a few days *before* you're licking the bottom of the salsa jar.

Time Spent: 15 seconds
Calories Expended: 3
Activity Level: 2

30. Apologize

If you explode in anger, at least clean up after yourself. A simple, "Sorry about that outburst. I will now return to my regularly scheduled pleasantness" will do the trick, and you barely have to exhale to say it. Acknowledging the error of your ways will save you untold amounts of time and effort too, in *not* having to deal with your friends' passive-aggressive emotional penalties going forward.

Time Spent: 10 seconds
Calories Expended: <1
Activity Level: 2

31. Don't Eat Your Roomie's Food

Poaching munchies uninvited is the lazy, cheap, and selfish trifecta. *Ask* if you can have one of those Devil Dogs, and your cohabitator will appreciate your consideration; maybe even enough to part with one of those delicious puppies. If they say no, work up the energy to go get your own, pay the insane fees to get them delivered or take a nap instead of stuffing your maw. This makes the world a better place and may ensure your own private hoard of Ho Hos remains undiminished.

Time Spent: Negative
Calories Expended: Negative
Activity Level: 1

32. Wear the Appropriate Clothing

Put on a clean shirt for work, even if you're remote. Cover that belly button for great grandma's 90th birthday party. In other words - dress for the occasion unless you want to be the main character in a *What Were They Thinking?* video. It's a cheap and easy way to show whoever's hosting the shindig that you respect them enough to bring your fashion flare down a degree. Since you're getting dressed anyway, this one costs you nothing.

Time Spent: Neutral
Calories Expended: Neutral
Activity Level: 1

SLAC-er Tip: How do you *know* what's appropriate? Ask the host, ask your boss, ask your mom. Or consult a full-length mirror. One of them will reveal the truth.

33. Say Excuse Me

Burp, bump or backside orchestra: basic politeness keeps society from crumbling into one big swamp of skunky behavior. Saying a simple, "Excuse me" gives you a patina of pleasantness instead of a lingering social stink, no matter what you did to require it. Oh yeah - bad puns definitely intended. Excuse me.

Time Spent: 5 seconds
Calories Expended: 1
Activity Level: 2

34. Does "Take More Naps" Count? Offer a Tip on Saving Energy

No, you don't have to think up an energy-saving tip on your own, lazybones. Feel free to share one you find in this book. Or online. Or wherever. Whether it's unplugging unused appliances or washing clothes in cold water, sharing your tip could inspire others to save energy too. *You* put in the same amount of effort, but the benefit grows exponentially. Now that's a lazy, selfish win if I ever saw one.

Time Spent: 30 seconds
Calories Expended: 2
Activity Level: 2

35. Slow Down and Go Around

My husband Tom and I used to live in Massachusetts, where the scenery is lovely, the infrastructure historic and the people active outdoors whenever the weather permits. The result? Thousands of runners, dog walkers, bicyclists, and bird watchers vying for space on roads constructed at roughly the time of the Salem Witch Trials. Having to *slow down* until I could zip around these people via the oncoming traffic lane used to drive me crazy. That is, until I realized it was usually a matter of a few seconds that I was trading for, you know, mutual safety. And, if I *hit* one of these folks, it would *really* mess up my day. Easier to get credit for being nice. So - slow down and, when safe, go carefully around.

Time Spent: 2 minutes
Calories Expended: 1
Activity Level: 2

36. Read an Etiquette Blog Then Be Etiquetty

Very few of us were *actually* raised by wolves, it's just that we're too lazy and selfish to worry much about manners. But now we're adults, and licking the plate at that rehearsal dinner just doesn't go over very well. Especially when it's not your plate. The good news? You can make yourself minimally mannerly from the comfort of your couch. Find an etiquette site that's right for you. Maybe it's the classic Emily Post Substack. If you're an Anglophile, or just more pretentious than average, try The Royal Butler. Maybe it's your dog that needs a little social upgrade. No need to expend a lot of energy, time or money; but *do* look for nuggets of civility that help you become slightly more polished when you have to be. You can sink into your usual dull luster every other day.

Time Spent: 2 minutes
Calories Expended: <1
Activity Level: 2

37. That Chocolate Fountain is Not a Party Favor

Leave Event Accessories at the Venue

At a wedding I attended several years ago, I was appalled to see more than one guest stuffing their purses (and *cars*) with anything that wasn't red hot or nailed down. Table linens. Folding chairs. Potted plants from the reception area. Anything and everything. The odd bottle of champagne tucked under a cummerbund I could understand, although I'm sure the bride and groom were *not* thrilled to pay for booze some selfish git quaffed in their hotel room. But - folding chairs? *Really*? You were the guest at an event, so play by the rules. If it's in a gift bag, has your name on it or is otherwise explicitly offered as a party favor, take it. If not? It's *stealing*, and you are way too selfish to share an 8'x10' cell with anybody.

Time Spent: Negative
Calories Expended: Negative
Activity Level: 1

38. Be Patient in the Grocery Checkout Line

I hate waiting in line for full-service grocery store checkout. But since I'm way too lazy to use the self-serve line, I *do* wait - and I used to be really nasty to others while I did it. To punish everyone for my self-inflicted frustration - because that makes sense - I used to sigh and sneer, roll my eyes and shift my weight so the checkout clerks, baggers and other customers could see exactly how much they were irritating me. What I realized? No matter how long it *seems* to take that customer ahead of me to figure out how to tap their debit card, it's almost *never* more than two extra minutes of my time. The DEFCON 5 emotional escalation isn't worth it - to anyone. My advice? Paste on a smile, visualize purring cats and mountain streams, and smugly calculate how much less energy *being patient* will burn.

Time Spent: 2 minutes
Calories Expended: Negative
Activity Level: 2

39. Move to the Middle of the Subway Car

Subways, airport monorails or other small, shared conveyances are often places for the selfish to shine - like bad pennies. Too often, it's like we were planted in the tube of movement, standing like sequoias in front of the door, forcing others to push past just to get *in* the thing. No matter that we've got 27 stops to go - we're selfish, and that means being *right by the door*. Every once in a while, make this the habit you break to make the world a better place. Move in toward the middle of the car, make space, and get credit for being civil while giving up exactly 24 inches of ground.

Time Spent: 5 seconds
Calories Expended: <1
Activity Level: 2

40. Try for Ten "Thank You's" Each Day

You'll find several ways to say "thank you" in this book; make a mental playlist of the ones you can use without breaking a sweat and put them on a loop. Thank the person who makes you your daily coffee. The person who holds the door open for you. Maybe toss a spare to a family member. Ten daily thank you's are almost as easy as breathing in and out, yet they give a teeny, tiny lift to ten people. Work your way up to a 2-minute commitment on this one by adding a specific compliment to the baseline thanks. Something like, "Thank you - I appreciate you putting all the papayas in one bag" is all it takes to make this a compendium of greatest kindness hits.

Time Spent: 2 minutes
Calories Expended: 3
Activity Level: 2

SLAC-er Bonus: To say "thank you" in sign language: Hold your fingers and palm open and flat in front of your face. Place the fingers of your hand, palm in, on your chin, then pull them away and toward the person you're thanking. Adding a smile, some eye contact, and a little nod would be nice too.

41. Participate in Other People's Milestones

Are you rolling your eyes, just a little, at the invite to your neighbor's kid's 4th grade graduation party? Grinding your teeth at that 6-month half-versary dinner you have to show up at? Keep it all inside. People celebrate what makes them happy, and they're inviting you along for the ride. There's no way to avoid attending, so do what comes naturally to your lazy self and go with the flow. You don't have to bring a gift, tightwad; but no snarking on social ahead of time, and no mean mumbling at the event. Show up with a sleepy Sometime Samaritan smile and congratulate the kid, the couple or whoever. Thank them for inviting you to share in their happiness. And? Here's a newsflash: your pals weren't thrilled to show up for Mr. Fuzzy's Cat-Mitzvah either, but they did. Now you're even.

Time Spent: Neutral
Calories Expended: Neutral
Activity Level: 1

42. It's Not Worth the Flipping Effort: Retire "The Bird"

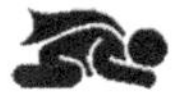

Isn't it amazing how many theoretical adults with responsible jobs, 401k's, and sensible shoes still deliver this one-fingered insult at the drop of a hat? Even though we all know that, at best, it has zero impact on the behavior of others. I've seen thousands of people get flipped off, but I've never once seen a flipee blush with chagrin, shape up their act, and apologize for whatever earned them the one-fingered wave. All the bird does is illustrate that you're willing to respond to some sort of crappy behavior with a tacky finger gesture. Unless of course you hit the jackpot, and the exchange results in the kind of cringey grownup fistfight we all doomscroll on TikTok. Why waste energy on something with a guaranteed negative ROI? As my mother-in-law Joyce used to say, it's not worth the flipping effort.

Time Spent: Negative
Calories Expended: Negative
Activity Level: 1

43. Practice At-Home Recycling

Fair: the recycling bins in most public places are too exacting for lazy people to deal with. If you're not already using them, you have my permission to ignore them forever. But, if you have a city recycling program that allows you to tip your takeout container into a recycling receptacle in your house, that's sitting right next to the "not recyclable" trashcan? Do it. One takeout container a day may not seem like much, but after a year you'll have stacked up enough plastic to act as a full-size sofa. If everyone in New York City alone recycled one container each day for that year, they would fill *5,000 apartments*. That's a skyline-sized pile of plastic!

Time Spent: 15 seconds
Calories Expended: 3
Activity Level: 2

44. Tell People When They're About to Forget Something

If you see someone about to leave the coffee shop without their debit card, sunglasses or bag of pine-apples - rouse yourself to give a quick shout. Yelling, "Hey! Did you mean to leave your iPad for that no-whip mocha lunatic heading for your former table?" barely requires an extra exhale. I mean, maybe they're just getting a napkin and will BRB. But if they drag their backpack to the front of the shop while the keys to a $90,000 vehicle are left sitting in the sticky, that person would probably appreciate the question. Ex-pending calories to pick whatever the thing is up and walk it over to its owner is too much to expect from someone as lazy and selfish as us. Hollering is enough.

Time Spent: 5 seconds
Calories Expended: <1
Activity Level: 2

45. Are You Thinking Something Nice? Say It!

Even selfish people like us have an occasional positive thought about another person. Imagine how good you could make that person feel if you just *said* that good thing when you thunk it? Whether it's, "I love that bracelet", "That pineapple salad was delicious", or "Your preso really got everyone thinking"; if positivity pops into your head, let it out. With the amount of effort it takes to, you know, *exhale*, you could make someone's day. Walk away quickly so you don't get bogged down in any tedious follow-up socializing.

Time Spent: 5 seconds
Calories Expended: <1
Activity Level: 2

46. Pet Your Pet

Throw a ball, dangle a string, or just give them a quick rub behind the ears. I'm not talking six hours at the dog park here - you can stay on the couch, I promise! But whether cat, canine, or ferret, showing two minutes of affection to your pet is a lazy and inexpensive way to nurture their well-being while selfishly gaining their affection forever. If you have a pet fish, I have no idea how that works - move on to the next suggestion.

Time Spent: 2 minutes
Calories Expended: 10
Activity Level: 3

47. Sorry, Just Seeing This!

Most of us lazy, cheap, and selfish people are familiar with getting called out for not calling back. Unresponsiveness is a core competency of the devotedly sluggish and self-absorbed. But - nobody needs to *feel* overlooked and insulted if you're willing to expend the tiniest bit of energy. So even if you saw that Slack days ago, buy yourself a reset and acknowledge their frustration with a quick apology and a teeny fib.

Time Spent: 3 seconds
Calories Expended: <1
Activity Level: 2

48. Lose That Resting Bad Face: Smile

Smiling is actually contagious - in a good way. If you smile at someone, chances are they will not only smile back at you but will *continue* smiling. Think of the implications. If you were to smile at someone first thing in the morning, it's possible you could trigger happy faces in your entire city by the end of the day! Because it lifts your face naturally, smiling can make you look both younger and thinner, with almost no effort - a SLAC-er trifecta.

Time Spent: 3 seconds
Calories Expended: <1
Activity Level: 2

SLAC-er Tip: If you usually walk around with a scowl on your face, practice turning up the corners of your mouth in front of the mirror to prevent unintentionally trading a frown for looking insane. That wouldn't make *anyone's* day better.

49. Focus Your Kiddo's Elimination Activities

Even the most lazy and selfish parent will do anything for their child. Perversely, this includes shielding them from the plague-ridden toilet seats of the revolting places we knowingly drag them into. But: do not hold your child in the general vicinity of the toilet and encourage them to use the entire stall as a canvas for their wee-wee. Either find restrooms where they can sit down without a hazmat suit or take the opportunity to strengthen your core by holding little Pubert closer to the commode. And cleaning up afterward.

Time Spent: 2 minutes
Calories Expended: 10
Activity Level: 3

50. Send Thank You Notes

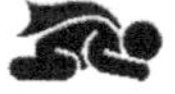

Did you know? You can get credit for making the world a better place even when it's because someone did something nice for *you*. It's called the Thank You Note. There's no need to go all Jane Austen with three paragraphs of gratitude on deckle-edged stationery (I'm too lazy to explain what a "deckle edge" is - ask Siri or Alexa if you really want to know). Just a quick text, "Thanks for arranging the game night" or "I appreciated the ride!" will get you karmic credit for making the world a better place. Since it's likely that this person did something you were too lazy, cheap, or selfish to do yourself, a quick TY really is the very least you can do. Even by *our* standards.

Time Spent: 1 minute
Calories Expended: 3
Activity Level: 2

51. "Everybody Say String!" Offer to Take Their Picture

That cute couple trying to get a selfie by the lake. The mom who would otherwise never appear in a family photo. The simple offer of "Do you want a picture with *all* of you in it?" is a terrific way to change the world for the better. And not only will you make strangers happy for a moment, you'll be remembered forever when they talk about that pic in Cawker City, Kansas. "Hey, that's us in front of the world's largest ball of twine! Wasn't it nice of that gal to wake up and take our picture?" A lazy, cheap way for a selfish person to go down in history.

Time Spent: 1 minute
Calories Expended: 5
Activity Level: 2

52. Nix the "X" Word

Whatever your swear word of choice - mine used to be "w&0#*" but recently I've been saying "s&!%" - hold back from bellowing it just once each day when you otherwise would've. Come up with a sound-alike you can substitute for The Nasty. Soon, you might find your Sometime Samaritan self in the habit of just - *not* swearing. If you were a real potty-mouth in the past, you may change the world dozens of times before lunch!

Time Spent: Neutral
Calories Expended: Neutral
Activity Level: 2

53. Greetings!

Saying hi, hey or howdy is a very easy way for lazy, cheap, and selfish people to interact with the world. It makes others feel seen, without the irritation or effort of actually having a conversation. Should the stranger you salute decide it's an open door to more chit-chat, you can decide whether to engage. But, between us, I give you permission to pretend that "Hello!" is the only word of their language you know.

Time Spent: 2 seconds
Calories Expended: <1
Activity Level: 2

54. Push in Your Chair

You're done eating. You stand up. Before heading home for your nap, push the chair up tidily to the table. It takes almost no effort and prevents other people from tripping, which certainly makes the world a better place. It also helps you avoid the time and effort it might take to sympathize. Or drive them to the emergency room.

Time Spent: 2 seconds
Calories Expended: 1
Activity Level: 2

55. Give Those Service Workers Some Love

They may not be a counter-service virtuoso or pizza-making protégé, but they are *there*. And they deal with people like us eight hours a day, so a little appreciation is justified. A quick "Thank you very much!" to cashiers, waitstaff, or delivery drivers acknowledges their work. This small gesture may brighten their day enough to keep them coming back to make your pizza, so you don't have to.

Time Spent: 2 minutes
Calories Expended: <1
Activity Level: 2

56. Backpacks Face Front When Boarding

When it's on your back, it's easy to forget what that 78-pound projectile you're swinging like Elvis's hips can do to someone's eyeglasses. Before you board that plane, train, or subway, rearrange your backpack as a frontpack so you can control it while you find your seat. It takes a tiny bit of effort, but it's more than offset by the financial gains of *not* having to replace the Panthere de Cartier sunglasses the gal in 29C is wearing.

Time Spent: 15 seconds
Calories Expended: 2
Activity Level: 2

57. It's a Doorbell, Not the Percussion Section: Ring Once, Then Wait

Not everyone has a smart doorbell/door cam, and not everyone who *does* have a smart doorbell/ door cam is ready to instantly engage the audio like a gunslinger at the OK Corral. Patience will make the world a better place. Hitting the doorbell like it owes you money doesn't make anyone move faster. In fact, you may even have to waste energy you don't have explaining why you thought 47 rings were necessary to get grandma to the door. One polite push every 10 seconds is enough.

Time Spent: Negative
Calories Expended: Negative
Activity Level: 1

SLAC-er Tip: Poked that doorbell twice and no answer? Go home. Grandma doesn't want to see you today.

58. Stop Leading with "Rescue"

Some of you are *really* good people - you rescued a dog or cat or even a lizard from the local shelter. Maybe more than one! And everyone admires you for doing it, including me. But please stop talking about it. There's awareness building, and then there's "Look how noble I am" posturing and "You're a jerk for buying a purebred" judgment. Don't be that rescuer. If someone asks, tell them your little Bingo is from a shelter. Otherwise, just tell them its name-o and thank them for complimenting your cherished pet.

Time Spent: Negative
Calories Expended: Negative
Activity Level: 1

59. Take Your Food Pic Fast - Or Not at All

It may be your thing – and more power to you! But nobody wants to watch you set up a photo shoot while their fries get cold. Snap your #foodiebragshot quickly - or skip it, when you're with a group of un-likeminded eaters. Then, you can all eat while the food still tastes like food. And get home for your naps.

Time Spent: Negative
Calories Expended: Negative
Activity Level: 1

60. Milton Wants His Swingline Back: Return Borrowed Work Tools

That stapler you borrowed? That pen you swiped from your colleague's desk? Take it back when you're done with it. Take. It. Back. Remember, you're going to want to borrow more stuff from these co-workers in the future. Returning the items you borrowed this time ensures that they're well-stocked when you hit them up next week. Want extra karmic credit? Break off a "Thank you for lending me that highlighter."

Time Spent: 1 minute
Calories Expended: 3
Activity Level: 2

61. Avoid Loud Entrances or Exits

You get up at 5am. Or, more likely, you're getting *in* at 5am. Your neighbors - not so much. Be kind to those who are still sleeping and close your apartment door gently. Don't bellow greetings into the house. No phone or other audio until you're inside your own four walls. Remember, the hallway is not an extension of your apartment. Also, whether parking lot or driveway: If you can see a neighbor's house, even in the misty distance - absolutely, positively no horn honking. You'll want your neighbors to do the same when you're sleeping off *your* Hulu binge.

Time Spent: Negative
Calories Expended: Negative
Activity Level: 1

62. Chew With Your Mouth Closed

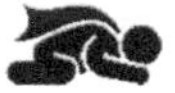

You think I wouldn't have to suggest this, but here we are. Make an effort to bring those lips together for quiet mastication. Smack-free chewing is a basic courtesy, so doing it whenever you remember counts as your SLAC-er good deed for the day. It makes everyone's life - or at least, lunch - a better experience. It also prevents them from asking you to share some of that yummy-looking Tuna Surprise.

Time Spent: Neutral
Calories Expended: Neutral
Activity Level: 1

63. Give the Easy Reference

No, I'm not asking you to write a detailed recommendation for a colleague - that's for those energetic, engaged world-changers. But when someone asks for a quick intro? Or you get that auto-reference request from LinkedIn? Type a few words or click a couple boxes - done. You're a hero to someone looking for a job and you didn't even break a sweat.

Time Spent: 2 minutes
Calories Expended: 3
Activity Level: 2

64. Praise a Friend's Creative Achievement

Have one of those annoyingly talented friends with the gumption to put the fruits of said talent out into the world? Leave a kind comment, share their link or otherwise give them some love. You don't have to write a novel just because they did. But maybe a Mad Libs for the lazy but sincere? "Hey [your audience]! Check out the incredible [creative thingy] my [relationship to subject], [subject], did. So proud of them!" You're now officially a patron of the arts.

Time Spent: 15 seconds
Calories Expended: <1
Activity Level: 2

65. Clean the Office Microwave

Someone's leftover tuna casserole exploded in the breakroom microwave? Four days ago? That is sooooo not your problem. Except you'd really like to heat up your lunch without it comingling with the tuna bits. Here's a radical thought: wipe that splatter disaster with a couple wet paper towels. It will take you under a minute to make a huge difference. Really. Don't believe me? Set a timer on your phone, employ your usual marginal cleaning techniques, and stop at sixty seconds. You'll be amazed. And, if that appliance is still a little disgusting, it's at least one minute less gross than it was. You're now the office hero and your delicious chicken soup doesn't reek of Chicken of the Sea.

Time Spent: 1 minute
Calories Expended: 10
Activity Level: 3

66. Don't Sigh

That expulsion of air you think is so subtle? It's an air horn of disdain. For whatever reason, you're listening to this person speak, so hold it together. If you must expel breath-bound irritation, hide it from the object of your scorn. Cover your mouth and let out a small cough instead of the in-your-face snarky sigh. You may even get some sympathy or allergy advice! Which could, in turn, result in them moving on from whatever sigh-inducing topic they were bloviating about.

Time Spent: Negative
Calories Expended: Negative
Activity Level: 1

67. Commemorate Their Milestone

Wish someone a happy birthday. Congrats on their anniversary. Kudos on Bucky's Cat-Mitzvah. You don't have to bake a cake or buy a present, you lazy tightwad. You don't even have to *remember* the milestone - social media will remind you. A two-second "Happy B-day!" makes people feel good and shows that you care, at least enough to send your lazy best.

Time Spent: 20 seconds
Calories Expended: 1
Activity Level: 2

68. Admit They Were Right

So you just discovered that the small intestine really *is* longer than the large intestine, eh? After having an actual argument with your second cousin's fiancée about it? Google and ChatGPT have greatly reduced this opportunity for strife, but it sadly hasn't disappeared. I'm amazed at how often friendships are ruptured over disagreements over insanely unimportant "facts." When you discover that someone was, in fact, *right* about something, you should tell them. You don't have to like it. You just have to *say* it: "You were right about that thing." It puts the universe back in balance and shows that you can be the bigger person. Like the small intestine.

Time Spent: 5 seconds
Calories Expended: 1
Activity Level: 2

SLAC-er Addendum: Unless someone you both really like is choking, or you're arguing about what the backpack for a zombie apocalypse happing *right now* should contain - ask AI and be done. Bow to whatever answer you get instead of spending the next four hours of your lives digging through original sources. You're *lazy*, remember?

69. Don't Sleep in Class

I'll say it: some instructors can make even interesting material a complete snooze-fest. With Sometime Samaritans being lazy and selfish to begin with, that can be a recipe for class disaster. But there's some reason why you're in this class, and some reason why this guy was picked to teach it, so be bare-minimum polite, at least. Keep your eyes open. You don't have to engage, just stay awake. You'll *look* engaged and invested while completely justifying your post-class nap. It's possible you'll also learn something, but that's up to you.

Time Spent: Neutral
Calories Expended: 10
Activity Level: 3

70. Obey the "Quiet Car" Train Rule

To less-lazy people, this falls under the category of Sayings from Captain Obvious: if you choose to sit in the designated quiet car of a train - *be quiet*. Quiet for real, not selfish-person quiet. Don't talk on your phone. Don't watch llama videos without your headphones on. Don't talk above a whisper. It's actually, you know, a *rule*. And you do *not* want to expend the extra energy to walk your lazy behind to another car when you get kicked out of this one.

Time Spent: Neutral
Calories Expended: Neutral
Activity Level: 1

71. Grab Coffee for a Co-Worker

Going to the break room anyway? Ask your cubicle-neighbor if they want a coffee or a water. Assuming it's free, of course; we Sometime Samaritans are sporadically kind, but we are *always* penny-pinchers. If it's a no-cost option to make the world a little better, go for it. Even the fusspot who asks you for a no-foam cappuccino with half a packet of raw sugar and a sprinkle of cinnamon doesn't inconvenience you for more than a couple minutes. And now - they owe *you* a trip!

Time Spent: 2 minutes
Calories Expended: 6
Activity Level: 3

72. Be an Enthusiastic Spectator

Whether it's your girlfriend's volleyball championship or your best bud's soccer game, it's time to rouse yourself to a little enthusiasm. So, clap. Whoop. Yell, "Nice shot!" You're already sitting there; why not make whoever you're watching feel like an MVP? It costs your cheap self no money and gets you big-time buddy points. Too self-absorbed to follow the action? Just do whatever the more-engaged spectators do. Since some games, like softball, can last forever in selfish-person time, this may be too much to ask. Solution: you have my permission to use up ten calories in well-placed well wishing, then spend the rest of the game in a smilingly supportive semi-doze.

Time Spent: Neutral
Calories Expended: 10
Activity Level: 3

73. Pass Along a Free Online Resource

I'm too lazy to tell you the whole story, but Tom is *still* sharing the YouTube video that taught him how to unclog our garbage disposal just before a Friendsgiving gathering several years ago. Do you know of a great how-to video? Share the link. Who knows how many of your friends are elbow-deep in the blade-riddled maw of their own kitchen woodchipper, digging out pulped spinach, *right now*?

Time Spent: 15 seconds
Calories Expended: <1
Activity Level: 2

SLAC-er Addendum: I can't find the link and Tom isn't home, so you're on your own for the garbage disposal. But I'm sorry, so the balance of karmic kindness is neutral.

74. Connect with Appropriate Physical Contact

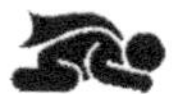

A little physical contact creates instant connection. Shake hands firmly. Hug warmly. Pat a shoulder kindly. These are fast, cheap, easy ways to make others feel good. Of course - keep it appropriate. We're trying to make the world a better, not creepier, place. I'm assuming you *know* these people.

Time Spent: 10 seconds
Calories Expended: 3
Activity Level: 2

75. I'll Take 5,000 Tic Tacs, Please: Buy in Tiny Bulk

Okay, so maybe 72 mega rolls of toilet paper are too much for your condo closet to handle. The good news? There is actually such a thing as a "tiny" bulk buy. Everything from Tic Tacs to tea bags come in refill or baby-bulk options that are small enough to fit in a corner of your sock drawer, allowing you to save the planet without feeling space deprived. And guess what else, tightwad? It's cheaper to buy this way. You're welcome.

Time Spent: 2 minutes
Calories Expended: 3
Activity Level: 3

SLAC-er Addendum: Don't store your Tic Tacs *or* your tea bags in your sock drawer.

76. Resolve the Service Stand-Off in Their Favor

I'm assuming you're not *so* selfish that you intentionally cut ahead of people who show up before you; but what do you do about the service standoff? When it seems like you and that other person ambled up at exactly the same time? The Sometime Samaritan way to resolve this is to let that person go first, however easy it would be for you to avoid eye contact and edge ahead. But, because we *are* lazy and selfish, I'm only asking you to do this at stores with more than one service person, so you don't end up waiting ten whole minutes while that person you let go ahead of you buys lunch meat for the Duggar family.

Time Spent: 2 minutes
Calories Expended: 5
Activity Level: 3

77. Lend a Hand

You don't have to lift the piano. But if someone's juggling a coffee, laptop and tote bag, grab their water bottle while they sort out their sherpa responsibilities. A few short seconds standing with a Stanley cup in your hand will ease their physical burden for a moment, and just maybe make their whole day seem a little brighter.

Time Spent: 1 minute
Calories Expended: 5
Activity Level: 3

78. Indulge Someone's Dream

When someone confides in you that they want to write a screenplay, open a bakery, or start a podcast about artisan pickles, here's a radical thought: just say, "That sounds interesting - I hope it's a huge success!" I'm not saying you should lie about their prospects, just resist the urge to roll your eyes or list the reasons why it'll never work. It costs you zero dollars to *not* be the person who kills their buzz.

Time Spent: 5 seconds
Calories Expended: 1
Activity Level: 2

79. Pull it Together: Don't Block the Moving Sidewalk

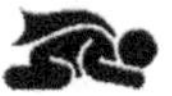

Those moving sidewalks are a lazy traveler's dream, but you don't want to be someone else's nightmare. Arrange your luggage, backpack, pineapples and pencil case so that you leave half the space for others to get past you. A *real* half, not a selfish-person's half. Preferably, organize your pile on the *right* side of the magic belt of movement and let the hustlers hustle past you on the left. You'll make the world a better place without even *moving*.

Time Spent: Neutral
Calories Expended: <1
Activity Level: 2

80. Compliment a Person's Pet

An easy way to make a pet owner's day is to compliment the little beast. Even if it's the weirdest wombat-looking hairball you've ever seen, there's got to be *something* redeeming about it. No? As a fallback, have a generic, neutral comment ready to say nicely. *"Look at that fur!"* said in a positive, cheery manner, for example, could mean anything - but you *made* it a compliment. And now both pet and owner are feeling good, without you having to even speak to the human. Yay you!

Time Spent: 3 seconds
Calories Expended: <1
Activity Level: 2

81. Deflect Mean Conversations

Hopefully, your natural laziness precludes you from *initiating* random discourse on why "those people" - or at least "their" candidates, culture or taste in socks - are idiotic. But what if you're face-to-face with someone who wants to go there? If someone you can't avoid at next week's Scrabble mixer burps out something derogatory, treat it like any other embarrassing bodily noise - ignore it. Pause, look up at the sky, then move the conversation back onto the path it was taking before the stink of snark appeared. If they don't take the hint? Try, "Oh, I was really hoping to catch up on what *you've* been doing instead of talking about politics/religion/sock choices. Tell me how little Pubert is!" Still burping? I recommend a well-timed choking fit and a quick exit to the next room.

Time Spent: Neutral
Calories Expended: 2
Activity Level: 2

82. Compliment Someone's Smile

A kind word about someone's smile not only boosts their confidence but also encourages more smiles all around. It's a small act with big rewards. "You have such a sunny smile!" is a nice, non-creepy way to say this to anyone.

Time Spent: 5 seconds
Calories Expended: <1
Activity Level: 2

83. Apologize - Yes, Even Though it Was an Accident

Maybe you cut in line accidentally, or spilled coffee on someone's backpack while absorbed in a video on okra pickling. It wasn't a Shakespearian betrayal, but the offended party has called you on it - maybe loudly or even rudely. Your best bet to make the world a better place while limiting your caloric burn? Stay calm and say, "You're right - I'm really sorry." No arguing, no justifying, no snark. You don't get world-changing points for acknowledging your own screw-up, but you *do* get credit for de-escalating a tense situation that, however inadvertently, you started.

Time Spent: 10 seconds
Calories Expended: <1
Activity Level: 2

84. Sitting Pretty (Lazy) at 814 Feet! Recommend a Helpful App

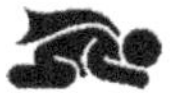

Whether it's SnapCalc, Daily Dad Jokes or Zoltar the Fortune Teller, everyone has a few apps they couldn't live without. If you have one you love, offer it up in the group chat. You've been helpful, engaged and generous in one fell swoop, and you didn't even have to wiggle your behind out of your beanbag to get it done.

Time Spent: 20 seconds
Calories Expended: <1
Activity Level: 2

SLAC-er Bonus: If you always want to know what elevation you're at, My Elevation is a great app for that. Yes, this *is* something many of us think about.

85. Cheer for Someone Else's Kid

Let's face it, t-ball coaching material we are not. Way too much time, effort and agita. So I'm not asking you to commit to a season, or even a whole game, of kiddie kindness. But giving some little cookie-crumbler a thumbs up or a "Great job!" when they cross home plate takes almost zero time or effort. And - karmic kindness plus - kids remember compliments from non-parental grownups forever. So do their parents.

Time Spent: 5 seconds
Calories Expended: 1
Activity Level: 2

86. Put Your Shopping Cart in the Cart Corral

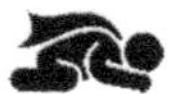

Loose carts are a menace to parking lots everywhere. Not to mention the huge hassle and possible monetary outlay for repairs if your cart-missile is seen ramming that Bentley. Next time you're getting ready to shove your shopping cart in the general direction of the cart corral and slip selfishly into your ride, be a grocery store hero and walk it *all the way* into the chute. It takes much less time and effort than you think. Yeah, I timed it.

Time Spent: 30 seconds
Calories Expended: 4
Activity Level: 2

SLAC-er Bonus: Want to count this one twice with zero extra effort? If your store's cart corral has specific chutes for smaller versus larger carts, put yours in the correct chute and you're done doing good for the *week*!

87. Know When to Leave Your Pet at Home

You love to take your faithful Bloodhound Hubert everywhere. But grocery stores, microchip factories, hospitals - they're a little hinky about you bringing your fur baby into the operating room. It's not because they don't love Hubert as much as you do, but there are actually *rules* about keeping pets out of certain spaces. It's possible the business could get fined if you bring along your pet, which definitely subtracts from your karmic world-changing score. It's also possible *you* could get fined - which would *really* mess up your day. And Hubert's. He'll get over being left behind if you bring him something nice from the gift shop.

Time Spent: Neutral
Calories Expended: Negative
Activity Level: 1

88. Thank Family Members as You Would Strangers

Making the world a better place can certainly begin at home. With that in mind - would you thank a stranger for passing the salt? Hint, the right answer is yes, you selfish animal. If you'd thank that rando, then thank your family member. This is a super easy world-changer, and will make a tiny dent in the family balance of goodness for all those chores you don't do.

Time Spent: 3 seconds
Calories Expended: <1
Activity Level: 2

89. Pick Up That Junk You Dropped

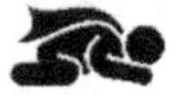

It's *your* junk, so you're just keeping the karmic scorecard in neutral by picking it up. Still - no lazy person wants to be digging themselves out of an existential hole, right? Combine some much-needed stretching with picking up that Nutrageous candy bar wrapper you just dropped. Grab it, toss it, and keep your saving-the-world scorecard on par while telling everyone you *worked out* today.

Time Spent: 2 seconds
Calories Expended: 1
Activity Level: 2

90. Like a Friend's Social Media Post

Here's one for the Sometime Samaritan minimalist: if a social-media pal posts something upbeat, funny or kind, give it a like, a laugh or a heart. One click, zero calories, and you've engaged in a positive way. It's the least effort you can put forward to keep your friendships from turning to dust. Not used to this whole making the world a better place thing? Start here.

Time Spent: 3 seconds
Calories Expended: <1
Activity Level: 2

SLAC-er Bonus: No friends? Been there. You can always go to Facebook or Instagram and like our stuff!

91. Say Hello to the Older Folks

Sometimes the older folks at festivities get overlooked by other guests - this is an opportunity for you to do some good by doing almost nothing. Just briefly greet the grandparents at a get-together and, trust me, it will make their day. Tell them who you are and ask how they're related to the hosts. Compliment a snappy shirt. You'll instantly become That Charming Young Person while spending less effort than it takes to open the Ensure. Remember, unless your family makes good on its threats, you will be older someday too.

Time Spent: 2 minutes
Calories Expended: 3
Activity Level: 3

SLAC-er Addendum: What's "older?" Don't worry about it - just greet people you think are your parents' or grandparents' age. Nobody like that in the room? You get a pass. But - maybe be prepared to be friendly to Some Charming Young Person who's working this suggestion at the same event.

92. Take That Whatever to Lost and Found

If you've ever lost something, you know the relief and happiness of getting it back, even if it was your backup-to-the-backup earbuds from 2018. It's a good thing to help reunite people with their lost stuff; especially if there's a way to do it that doesn't make us work too hard. That's what's great about any place with a Lost and Found bin - no need to hire a detective or hang up fliers on the light posts. You just pick up that Homer Simpson keychain, walk it over to the receptable, drop it in and walk away. So do it. The universe will notice.

Time Spent: 2 minutes
Calories Expended: 5
Activity Level: 3

93. Make Room for Others

There's nothing we selfish people like better than taking up enough room for three defensive linemen on any flat surface we perch on. It's just more comfortable that way; and we have room to stretch out for our nap if it gets to be that time. But *not* doing it is a prime opportunity to make the world a better place without spending any extra money, time or effort. So, if there's room for others - or their junk - on the bench or table, give it over. You don't have to like it, but it *will* get whoever is standing there giving you the stink eye out from in front of you.

Time Spent: 3 seconds
Calories Expended: 1
Activity Level: 2

94. Oh Mr. Coffee... Make the Next Pot

You just took the last, sludgy cup of coffee from the communal pot. Now the Coffee Fairy will magically replenish it! But you know that's not real, right? Right? Brewing the next pot of coffee is a way to get your world-changing brownie points in for the day *and* avoid working at the same time. Yay – a twofer! By the way, this counts at home too.

Time Spent: 2 minutes
Calories Expended: 5
Activity Level: 3

95. Shut the Curtains on Hot/Cold Days

If the temperature is north of 90 or south of 30 degrees Fahrenheit, shutting the curtains or blinds can be the almost-no-effort gesture you make that keeps your city's entire electrical grid from going down. And, of course, it makes it much easier to nap. Extra karmic points for you if you don't demand a key to the city from your mayor.

Time Spent: 2 minutes
Calories Expended: 5
Activity Level: 3

96. Consider Concentrates

Take an extra 15 seconds to find the "concentrated" or "refill" version of whatever liquid thingy it is you're about to buy, from hand soap to cold brew. This is an itty-bitty world saver, because concentrates can have up to 99% less packaging than the ready-to-use replacement. A SLAC-er bonus? They're often a lot cheaper than ready-to-use, which will make your skinflint instincts sing. And yes, I timed it – replenishing with a concentrate versus dragging out an entirely new bottle will barely put a dent in your precious scroll time.

Time Spent: 2 minutes
Calories Expended: 3
Activity Level: 3

97. Send a Picture

How can you do some passive good while lolling on a lounge chair scrolling your old photos? Send what you see. Forwarding a photo of you and your BFF at the 2017 Crocheting Festival with a quick "This made me think of you!" reminds your friends that you actually *do* care about them. And here you were, thinking you weren't *doing* anything today.

Time Spent: 20 seconds
Calories Expended: 1
Activity Level: 2

98. Let Them Brag

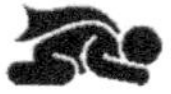

If you want to actually *have* friends, you will have to let them tell their stories sometimes without throwing shade or tuning out. The memory of their half-marathon completion or win of the Miss Pickle title may get on your very last selfish nerve, but friends let friends brag a little. So smile. Nod. Give them some love. If they can't wind it up in a couple minutes, you have my blessing to pretend a bug flew into your eye, but otherwise just bask in their reflected glory for a hot second.

Time Spent: 2 minutes
Calories Expended: 2
Activity Level: 2

99. Wave to Neighbors

When Tom and I moved to the town where we live now, our realtor drove us around the neighborhood where we eventually bought our house. As we drove, she returned the waves of everyone we passed. Tom remarked, "You certainly know a lot of people in this neighborhood!" Our realtor looked at us with deep pity in her eyes and said, "Actually, I don't know *any* of those folks. We're just waving to be nice. Don't you wave to each other where you live now?" Uh, actually – no. What a simple way to make the world a better place! A wave covers your minimum neighborly obligation without having to cross the street, chat, or even stop walking. This is something even the laziest SLACer can get into.

Time Spent: 3 seconds
Calories Expended: 2
Activity Level: 2

100. Tell Someone They're Doing a Great Job

Did a work colleague create a great marketing campaign? Or maybe your mechanic figured out what was making that whingy noise in your Vespa? You don't have to break a sweat writing a detailed performance review. Just say, "Hey - great job making that whingy noise go away!" Add a little enthusiasm and a sunny smile, and you've changed that person's world for the better, at least for a few minutes.

Time Spent: 10 seconds
Calories Expended: <1
Activity Level: 2

101. Stand to the Right on the Escalator

Not everyone stands still on the escalator like it's a ride at the world's most languid State Fair. If you're not going to walk up (and we all know you're not), stay to the right so others can pass you. If you let more energetic others move at their more speedy speed, you can doze another three to five seconds without someone breathing down your neck.

Time Spent: Neutral
Calories Expended: <1
Activity Level: 1

102. Compliment Great Service Providers

Yeah, it's their job to pour your coffee. But what if they're really good at it? Maybe they add just that little bit of flair that cuts through your sleepy semi-doze to bring *you* joy. It would be nice to reinforce that, wouldn't it? A quick compliment like "Love the smiley-face in my cappuccino foam!" to a barista or "So great you have a charger in the car!" to a rideshare driver earns you excellent world-changing karma - and might even get you extra foam or help with your luggage. Just remember that's not why you're doing it. Today, anyhow.

Time Spent: 5 seconds
Calories Expended: <1
Activity Level: 2

103. Getting Up Soon Anyway? Give Up Your Seat Now

If someone who just boarded seems to have some energy-sapping challenge, offer up your seat on the subway or bus. Let's not get crazy here. If you have a 30-minute ride ahead of you, avoid eye contact, hunker down, and stay seated. But if you're getting off at the next stop anyway? Change the world for the better, just by getting up a little early.

Time Spent: 2 minutes
Calories Expended: 10
Activity Level: 3

104. Offer Particular Praise to Your Instructor

Did you learn something new in that class today? Make a note and mention it specifically to your instructor. Whether it was inspiring, funny, new or useful; it will give this knowledge worker a metaphorical fist-bump of validation if you say so. The particulars are important in this case, because *attention* is one of the biggest compliments you can pay an educator. And, they'll be so surprised you were listening that you won't have to stick around for a deeper conversation.

Time Spent: 15 seconds
Calories Expended: 1
Activity Level: 2

105. Don't Throw Trash Out Your Car Window

Flinging that burrito wrapper out of your car window isn't just lazy and selfish - it's *publicly* lazy and selfish. Everyone sees you being nasty to the universe at large in a way that takes more energy and effort than just - not. It's not like you're getting rid of evidence - keep your garbage in your car until you get to a trash can.

Time Spent: Negative
Calories Expended: Negative
Activity Level: 1

106. Congratulate Colleagues on Career Milestones

Slow down - you don't even have to *stop* - on your way to the breakroom and snap out a quick "Great news about your promotion!" Too much? Click the Applause icon and the suggested *"Congrats!"* response on their "new gig" post on LinkedIn. Two twitches of your index finger and you've been gracious and kind. These minimal niceties also keep your name front-and-center in case they or their colleagues have another job opening. A career win-win.

Time Spent: 5 seconds
Calories Expended: 1
Activity Level: 2

107. Unplug a Device Not in Use

Did you know all those appliances tethered to your electrical outlets are using power even when they're *off*? It's called, "vampire power," and it's definitely sucking dollars out of your wallet. While this is an affront to cheapskates everywhere, it's also an opportunity to make the world a better place by doing almost nothing. Save some energy for others: unplug those watt-suckers and save the planet, one lava lamp at a time. And yes, I've accounted for all the effort it will take you to plug them back *in* when you want to use them.

Time Spent: 2 minutes
Calories Expended: 5
Activity Level: 3

SLAC-er Bonus: Connect devices that would normally be plugged in to hard-to-reach outlets through a power strip. That way, you can easily get your hands on the kill-switch and slay that power-sucking appliance activity.

108. I Have No Opinion - I'll Just Complain About Whatever You Decide: Participate in Your Own Plans

Participating in group planning goes against everything natural in your SLAC-er nervous system. *You're* not going to organize that reunion afterparty - but someone will. And you're bound to get asked about the venue, food and timing. If you plan to grace these festivities with your presence, respond to requests for ideas quickly and positively. Instead of "whatever," or dead air, how about "My first choice is Feral Pizza, but I'm happy to go wherever the group chooses. XO for arranging this!" If you respond to even one question in this engaged and appreciative way, you've made the world a better place *and* hung on to the few people in the world willing to hang out with you for at least another couple weeks. Not to mention having at least a shot at going someplace you actually *want* to eat.

Time Spent: 15 seconds
Calories Expended: 1
Activity Level: 2

109. Head to the Back of the Elevator

Standing right in front of the elevator doors even though others are coming on is lazy and selfish - behavior I respect. But taking just two steps backward racks up a tiny kindness in your Sometime Samaritan tally. I mean, c'mon - it's an *elevator*, not a jumbo jet. You'll get off exactly one nanosecond later than the people at the front. Besides, when were you *ever* in such a big hurry to get to work?

Time Spent: 5 seconds
Calories Expended: 1
Activity Level: 2

110. Reminisce with Relatives

Be honest - how often do you say something ***nice*** about one of your relatives? Wouldn't it make the world a better place to appreciate those branches on the family tree who still speak to you? Keep it simple, and stick to stories that don't trigger family drama. Something like, "Uncle Jack taught me how to fish. I caught my first bluegill and was - heh heh - hooked! It was really nice of him." Just avoid sharing this story with Aunt Dana if you know she thinks Uncle Jack is pond scum.

Time Spent: 1 minute
Calories Expended: 2
Activity Level: 2

111. Avoid the Restraining Order Leash Your Dog

Of *course* your lovely Tasmanian devil / coyote mix doesn't bite. But Fluffy is a little intimidating when she's hurtling toward a toddler at 45 miles per hour, so keep her on a leash wherever she might confuse humans with food. Sometimes it's actually a *rule* to muzzle your mastiffs, but it's also the considerate thing to do. Besides, can you imagine the legal expenses if your unassuming ball of gristle actually *does* chomp that kiddo? Not to mention the hassle of the trial, and moving towns, and dealing with the press. Nobody needs that.

Time Spent: 2 minutes
Calories Expended: 5
Activity Level: 3

112. Feeling Energetic? Return That Dropped Whatever to its Owner

Warning: this suggestion is not for the faint of heart. You may actually have to - accelerate. *And* interact. But snapping up those dropped keys, cash card or kumquats and putting on a little speed to return them is a high-payoff karmic kindness. And - big bonus alert - you've now burnt enough calories to completely justify a second nap.

Time Spent: 30 seconds
Calories Expended: 8
Activity Level: 3

113. Proactively Offer the Whatever

Don't wait to be asked - offer to pass the salt, guava jelly, coconut aminos - whatever. When you're done sprinkling and drizzling, ask if anyone else needs some and hand it over. You could be *really* polite and offer that cranberry mustard to your dining-mates *before* you take a crack at it, but I know who I'm dealing with here. It's enough that you didn't stash it in your bag so you could guzzle it all yourself.

Time Spent: 5 seconds
Calories Expended: 2
Activity Level: 2

114. Take a Shorter Shower

Nobody needs a 20-minute shower unless they're recording a shampoo commercial or washing off gunshot residue. But we're selfish, so I won't get too greedy. Cut just *one minute* off your daily ablutions, take one "speedy shower" each week or, if you're not particularly prone to stinkiness, skip one shower entirely every couple weeks. Save a little water and get an extra minute or two of sleep! A SLAC-er win/win.

Time Spent: Negative
Calories Expended: Negative
Activity Level: 1

115. Don't Block the Aisle

Whether store, office, or bowling alley - if you stop to scroll, stare, or take a nap, step out of the main flow of traffic first. Get someplace where you're not standing between two harried moms and the last jar of artisanal artichoke baby food. This Sometime Samaritan sorta-kinda kindness may also prevent an irritating shoulder bump just as you're really getting into that pickling video.

Time Spent: 5 seconds
Calories Expended: 1
Activity Level: 2

116. Put Your Towels in the "Used Towel" Bin

At the gym or at the pool, there's usually a bin, bag or bucket for those six damp towels you selfishly hogged up. They made a lovely cocoon, but now it's time to do right by them, the staff and your fellow sunbathers. Put them where they belong, so they'll be fluffy and clean for your next visit. Oh, and for those other people, too.

Time Spent: 15 seconds
Calories Expended: 3
Activity Level: 2

117. Don't Correct People

Yeah, okay – selfishly? Hearing my cousin use a double negative or a bestie say "I could care less" can blow my selfish equilibrium for the day. But correcting someone publicly makes you look worse than the mistake. If it's your kiddo who made the error, wait until you're alone together to make sure they know that *figuratively* is what they *literally* meant. Not your spawn? Not your purview. Kindly spare others the embarrassment - and yourself the effort - of being the human red pen. I mean really – do you *want* to spend your limited energy debating the Oxford comma? I didn't think so.

Time Spent: Negative
Calories Expended: Negative
Activity Level: 1

118. Stop Texting During Transactions

Paying for your coffee? Tapping your train ticket? Stop the doomscrolling for a few seconds and focus on what you're doing IRL. Chances are, it will speed up the transaction – a win for your selfish self - and ensure that you actually *take* that $9 Strato you just paid for. What about the "making the world a better place" part? The human who just served you, and the people waiting behind you, feel considered, if not actually appreciated. It really is the least you can do.

Time Spent: 30 seconds
Calories Expended: <1
Activity Level: 2

119. Make Eye Contact

Here comes your mom with a question. Your colleague with an update. Some rando asking where you got that pineapple. Yeah, I know – you don't want to talk to them. You want the whole interaction over with as soon as possible. What better way than to keep your eyes glued to that baby goat video? But this is an opportunity to show that you prioritize people over screens. Which you do. You don't have to fall in love; just glance up long enough to respond, give a quick smile, and move on. Kindness complete!

Time Spent: Neutral
Calories Expended: Neutral
Activity Level: 1

120. Compliment Someone's Outfit

Throwing out a quick "Love your shoes!" is a great way to lift someone's spirits without breaking a sweat. No, it's not like volunteering at the local food bank. But it *is* a SLAC-er gift that keeps on giving: a quick hit of happy feels for them now, and something to make them smile every time they slip on those Chuck Taylors.

Time Spent: 3 seconds
Calories Expended: <1
Activity Level: 2

121. Allow Someone to Merge into Traffic

Here's one, Sometime Samaritan: how about letting that car that's been sidling up beside you for the past 20 yards merge into the main flow of traffic? According to whatever source AI used to give me the answer, a Ford Escape, currently the most popular sedan in the U.S., is 15 feet long. That means you can get legit karmic kindness points by giving up just a few inches of your life. Letting one car in at a busy merge extends your commute by about 10 seconds - not a lot. Especially if you balance those 10 seconds with the emotional tension and caloric burn you waste maneuvering to intentionally block them out.

Time Spent: 10 seconds
Calories Expended: <1
Activity Level: 2

122. Since You're Exhaling Anyway . . . Say "Please" When Asking for Something

Politeness isn't just for kindergarteners. No, really. Puffing out a "please" in addition to whatever you're about to ask for ups the pleasantry and barely registers on the Activity Meter. So next time, it's "*please* pass the papayas."

Time Spent: 1 second
Calories Expended: <1
Activity Level: 2

123. Take a Message

A good one. It's not often that any of us *have* to take a message by hand, so doing it well gives you bragging rights while expending almost no effort. Write or enter the name of the caller/visitor, their contact information, when they called and what they want. The process is only finished when you actually *deliver* the message to the intended recipient. Even with the most long-winded caller, you should be able to wrap this up in under two minutes.

Time Spent: 2 minutes
Calories Expended: 2
Activity Level: 3

124. Take Up One Seat for Every Behind You Have

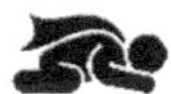

No, your backpack does *not* need its own seat, and yes, the bus/train/boat *is* going to be full. Put your crap on the rack above, under the seat in front of you or on your lap so other humans can sit. Still hesitating? It's totally okay to time your considerate clear-out to happen *after* that person you can smell coming down the aisle has passed your row.

Time Spent: 5 seconds
Calories Expended: <1
Activity Level: 2

125. Pass Group Goodies to Others First

I know, we've all seen the *Office Space* clip where Milton gets cheated out of the office birthday cake. But, one selfish person to another, I expect *you* to be able to do a quick count of whatever goodies are on offer so that The Big Cheat doesn't happen to you. It's kind to offer the goodie plate to a few others first, or pass the first couple cake slices that come your way before initiating the selfish snatch-and-snarf that is our usual MO. You'll still get a treat, but now you look like the generous, classy person in the room. Who knows? You may get promoted, or at least get to keep your Swingline stapler.

Time Spent: 1 minute
Calories Expended: 2
Activity Level: 2

126. Give Their Big Life Post Some Love

Engagements, pregnancy announcements, new jobs or new pets - these are a big deal for *anyone*. Since you've committed to being friends with these people, you owe it to them to sit up for a minute and type an actual "Congrats." In fact, I expect you to type the *whole word*. Muster up a little enthusiasm. You could even go the Sometime Samaritan version of the extra mile and expand a bit. Use a few exclamation points. Add a sentence or two of detail like, "Oh wow! Congratulations! So happy you and Fluffy decided to get a puppy!" It costs nothing and keeps you on the "just barely decent" friend list for another day.

Time Spent: 1 second
Calories Expended: <1
Activity Level: 2

127. Just Working Out How to Change the World:

Wipe Down Your Exercise Machine

What do you hate more than cleaning up your own puddle of liquid salt? Splashing down in someone else's. So think about others and do a quick wipey-wipey of that elliptical you've been leaning on for the past 15 minutes. You can then feel totally justified giving someone lazier and more selfish than you the side-eye when they don't. And - bonus - a couple more calories burned!

Time Spent: 15 seconds
Calories Expended: 5
Activity Level: 2

128. Don't Text While Walking

Not forever - you're selfish, and I sympathize. But for two minutes on any given day, look up from your phone and experience the thrill of seeing where you're going. Who knows, you may even discover a great new place to get your nails done. And, for 120 seconds, you'll cease to be the walking hazard that makes your fellow amblers want to scratch your eyes out.

Time Spent: 2 minutes
Calories Expended: Neutral
Activity Level: 1

129. Pump the Brakes When Someone Cuts You Off in Traffic

I've seen people pull into store parking lots *miles* from the Scene of the Incident to have it out over the epic "You cut me off!" scenario. I once saw a pistol waved. Really? This is an awful lot of effort for a lazy person. This suggestion is where we make the world a better place by not making it worse. When some jerk cuts you off in traffic - let it go. Don't do *anything* except slow down enough to make sure you don't get jammed up in the inevitable fender bender. Make this a go-to suggestion, if only because you're selfish enough to not want your obituary to read, "Died in a middle-aged slapfight over who should've merged onto I-35 first."

Time Spent: Negative
Calories Expended: Negative
Activity Level: 1

130. Complete the Feedback Form When You Have Something *Positive* to Say

You know it's true - no survey is too long when we have complaints. It's amazing how we can galvanize our lazy selves to deliver superlative spurts of vitriol when our pizza place forgets the pineapple. But when things go well? Yawn, too sleepy to say something nice. If you complete just *one* positive survey when you're feeling the love, you could not only make someone's day - you could secure their bonus or even their continued employment. Bonus points if you mention a service superhero by name!

Time Spent: 2 minutes
Calories Expended: 3
Activity Level: 3

SLAC-er Tip: AI can help you create an awesome "Slimy Dan's kelp-n-kale hamburger is a taste explosion!" review in record time, if you're too lazy to come up with such sparkling wit yourself.

SLAC-er Alternative: Just can't muster up the energy to bliss out in a full-blown rave response? I feel that. If it's too much to ask of your index fingers, skip the review but click five stars or whatever the top rating is - it's just barely better than nothing.

131. When You Care Just Enough to Send Something:

Communicate During Crises

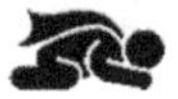

Do you have a friend who's going through a break-up? Job loss? You may be too selfish and lazy to lean into meaningful sympathy, but you *do* care, and you want them to know it. A quick text "You've been on my mind - I hope things are going better" with a hug emoji can mean, well, not a lot, but a *little*. It's an easy way to show someone they're marginally cared for. You can even put reminders on your calendar to do a few follow-up check-ins if it's, like, your mom or something.

Time Spent: 10 seconds
Calories Expended: 1
Activity Level: 2

132. Close the Cabinet, Close the Drawer

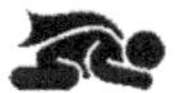

You opened it, now close it. It's just that simple. The cabinet door doesn't close itself. Open cabinets and drawers are the hazard of kitchens and offices everywhere. Remember, no matter how much effort it feels like to push that drawer panel a couple inches, it definitely takes less effort than the ER visit.

Time Spent: 2 seconds
Calories Expended: <1
Activity Level: 2

133. Clean Up After Your Dog

The street is deserted. Bingo takes a major D. You could just walk away. Don't. Your neighbors love your dog, they really do. But it's your dog, so it's your poo. Pick it up. Every. Single. Time. Besides, Mr. Wilson's Ring cam caught the whole thing, so you and Bingo are already busted.

Time Spent: 15 seconds
Calories Expended: 2
Activity Level: 2

134. Share an Inspirational Quote

Ever seen a quote and thought, "Huh - that's exactly how I feel"? Sharing that wisdom is a super-easy way for Sometime Samaritans to make a connection with people you care about and make their world a better place without breaking a sweat. It's fast, free, and lets you sound wise without actually having an original thought. Want to do this proactively? Probably not, but just in case: AI is full of ideas - just ask.

Time Spent: 1 minute
Calories Expended: 2
Activity Level: 2

SLAC-er Bonus: One of my faves is this quote from Lao Tzu, a 6th-century Chinese philosopher, who said "Doing nothing is better than being busy doing nothing." It's the perfect SLAC-er motto!

135. Wipe it Up

Yeah, okay - it's just a little dribble. A drop of coffee. A splash of water, even. What's the big deal? Selfishly, I can totally see just leaving whatever it is to dry up on its own. Because it *will*. But spilled liquids like coffee and soda stay sticky for a long time, maybe even coming back to haunt you when your sleeve drags through a mess of your own making. Even puddles of plain water can be a problem, as anyone who's ever put their $1,800 phone down to wash their hands knows. So, grab a sponge or other sopping utensil and do a quick wipe-up of the offending liquid. Then you can be on your selfish way knowing you made the world a better, and ever-so-slightly cleaner, place.

Time Spent: 15 seconds
Calories Expended: 5
Activity Level: 3

136. Give a Shout Out for Ongoing Kindness

From the mentor who answers our crazy work questions to the life partner who makes the bed every day; we lazy, cheap and selfish people often forget to thank those who do nice things for us on a daily basis. Think of the surprise these unsung heroes will feel - not to mention the happiness - if you pick a day to say, "Hey - it's really great of you to do this all the time. I don't say so often enough, but I really appreciate it!" Hint - put it on your calendar to say thanks for this thing every 3-6 months, to keep up the kind work.

Time Spent: 10 seconds
Calories Expended: <1
Activity Level: 2

SLAC-er Addendum: Thank you, Tom, for making the bed every day. It's really great of you to do it. I don't say so often enough, but I appreciate it!

137. Salute Military Personnel for Their Service

They volunteer to keep us safe from all manner of bad actors; the least we can do is acknowledge it when they're standing right there. Tom, who is only marginally less lazy, cheap and selfish than I am, is particularly good about doing this. A simple, heartfelt, "Thank you for your service" is all it takes to let those who risk their lives for us know they're appreciated, even by those of us who expect to be thanked for putting the toilet seat down.

Time Spent: 10 Seconds
Calories Expended: <1
Activity Level: 2

138. "Compost" is Just Another Way to Say "Lazy Trash"

You may have justified flinging that apple core to the ground as Earth-friendly because it's "compost" or will feed the wildlife. Wrong move, hippie. Yes, your banana peel *will* decompose - eventually. But on the sidewalk, it's *litter*. And gross. So, hang onto it until you get to the next trash can. If the thing you're about to drop is, truly, compostable, as banana peels and apple cores *are*, take it home with you and compost it for real. Yeah - I didn't think so.

Time Spent: 1 minute
Calories Expended: 6
Activity Level: 3

139. Don't Honk Your Horn

Don't honk your horn even if the idiot in front of you really, really deserves it. Your car horn is a warning device, *not* a therapeutic outlet or tool of public insult. And when has the "insult honk" ever changed the insultee's behavior one iota? Just don't, and make the world a better place with your sweet silence. Here's the selfish bonus: you actually *save* the effort you would've wasted on the honking. And the fistfight. And jail.

Time Spent: Negative
Calories Expended: Negative
Activity Level: 1

SLAC-er Tip: If you really, really don't want to miss out on expressing your traffic tantrum, yell "HOOOOONK!" instead of actually honking your horn. It will do exactly as much good, without you having publicly exposed yourself as a lunatic. Only the people in the car with you will know for sure.

140. Tell Someone They're Important to You

Whether family member or friend for life, these are the peeps you want to keep, so break off a little overt sentiment. If you've got those vibes flowing, let them out to spread the joy. It may be more emotional exposure than you're ready for, so feel free to fake a sneezing fit and run for the nearest nap room if either of you starts getting teary.

Time Spent: 2 minutes
Calories Expended: <1
Activity Level: 3

141. Offer Kudos for Adopting a Rescue Pet

While you get karmic credit by not mentioning that *your* pet is a rescue, that doesn't mean you shouldn't drop a little love on someone who felt the need to put it out there. A quick "great of you to rescue!" is an easy, cost-effective way to make them feel validated. Because, after all, they *did* do one of those big things that make the world a better place.

Time Spent: 3 seconds
Calories Expended: <1
Activity Level: 2

142. Pick Up a Piece of Litter

The bend and - snap! for discarded crap is a good one to do someplace where trash cans are close by - I don't expect SLAC-ers like me to drag somebody's discarded gum wrapper to the ends of the earth. Yeah, yeah - it's not *your* trash, so why is this your job? As a selfish and lazy person myself, I get it. But remember, you're trying to get credit for making the world a better place. Binning some *other* lazy, selfish person's Poppi can transforms you into Captain Planet and takes almost no time or effort. Of course, if it's oozing or otherwise stinkish, you have my blessing to move on to good-deeding with something less gross.

Time Spent: 1 minute
Calories Expended: 5
Activity Level: 3

143. Send a Virtual Hug Emoji

Sending a virtual hug when one of your peeps does something huggable makes your online world just that little bit more pleasant. The hug-by-proxy has a great effort-to-payoff ratio. The emoji does the hugging, and you get to change the world just a just a hair, without leaving the couch.

Time Spent: 2 seconds
Calories Expended: <1
Activity Level: 2

144. Thanks for the Reco

Someone went out of their way to give you a recommendation on a book, game or podcast they heart, which you engaged with and hearted too? Give them a little love back with a quick text saying why. "Oh man - I loved *No Such Thing as A Fish!* They had an episode on honey badgers, and you know how much I heart honey badgers!"

Time Spent: 30 seconds.
Calories Expended: 1
Activity Level: 2

SLAC-er Addendum: Didn't love it? Okay to say so, just acknowledge the kindness behind the suggestion. "I didn't dig *Digging,* but thanks for unearthing it for me!"

145. Praise Something Unique About Someone Else's Kid

If you're not too lazy, find a standout something about someone else's kid that you can praise sincerely. Extra points if the kid maybe isn't the basketball team's superstar or perennial science-fair winner. "It's so cool that Austin always helps clean up the snack trash" or "Willa stays so focused in games!" It will make a parent's day - and you have my permission to feign a pressing appointment if they try to angle for more.

Time Spent: 15 seconds
Calories Expended: 2
Activity Level: 2

146. Replace the Toilet Paper Roll

I know. You didn't use the last square. Well, okay, you *did*, but you need all your energy to get back to the couch. Just every once in a while, make the effort to go get a new roll and be a hero to whoever is bathroom-bound next. Extra points if you actually put the roll *on* the holder instead of perching it precariously on the back of the toilet tank.

Time Spent: 30 seconds
Calories Expended: 3
Activity Level: 2

147. Let Someone Go Ahead in Line

The person behind you in the grocery line has, like, two pineapples and some shaving cream. But it's almost naptime, and you're in what passes for a hurry with people like us. What to do? Letting them go ahead of you in the checkout line is an easy way to make the world a better place while you just stand there for another couple minutes.

Time Spent: 2 minutes
Calories Expended: <1
Activity Level: 2

148. Stop your Car to Let Someone Cross the Street

One skill that's been very helpful in writing this book: the ability to count seconds. "One-one thousand, two-one thousand..." and you can find out how "interminable" many irritating life scenarios are. Turns out, most of them terminate much more quickly than our selfish selves think. Stopping to let a pedestrian amble across the road or parking lot in front of you, for example. Even people as lazy as us can usually manage it in under 15 seconds - normal people barely ever take more than seven. You can be kind while giving up less than a quarter-minute of your life. Sounds like a pretty good deal to me!

Time Spent: 10 seconds
Calories Expended: <1
Activity Level: 2

149. Let Them Win the Phone Face-Off: Stop Scrolling When Conversing with a Live Human

Let me get this straight: some living person right in front of you is willing to interact with your selfish self and you're shopping yoga pants on lululemon? Either go directly home and brick yourself in or put. The phone. Down. Look up - nod, even. Either engage with this person who is trying to connect with you or tell them you're late for your flatulence support group and go scroll someplace else.

Time Spent: Neutral
Calories Expended: Negative
Activity Level: 1

150. Acknowledge the "Have a Good Day!"

You've just picked up your deli order. As your slippers are scuffing toward the exit, the guy behind the counter says, "Have a good day!" To which you reply with the sound of one deli door, closing. Yeah, it's rote. Yeah, they might not even *care* if you have a good day. But a quick and cheery "You too!" finishes the interaction on a high note. There's almost nothing you can do to make the world a better place with less effort. Not that I won't keep looking.

Time Spent: 2 seconds
Calories Expended: <1
Activity Level: 1

151. Choose Digital Over Printed Receipts

I mean, what? Like you're going to *save* those paper receipts and keep track of your purchases in case you need to take something back in 17 days? I didn't think so. Say yes to digital, save a few trees, and avoid the effort of having to dispose of 43 tiny, faded little paper twists that are stuffed into your car console. The side bennie? Your phone will do the saving for you, and who knows? You may actually go get that refund on that can of expired tuna.

Time Spent: Neutral
Calories Expended: Neutral
Activity Level: 1

152. If You Sprinkle...

Ladies, you know who you are. We have the opportunity to make the public bathroom a better (and *waaaaay* more hygienic) place by simply peeing like we would if we were at home. If the venue you're in is so foul that you're afraid of putting your bottom on the toilet seat - what are you *doing* there? Either wait until you get home, wear Depends or bring surgical gloves and cleaning supplies to tidy up your tinkle. Here's a thought - maybe it wouldn't *be* so disgusting if we all just, you know - *sat down*.

Time Spent: 10 seconds
Calories Expended: 3
Activity Level: 2

153. Return the Household Item to Its Rightful Spot

Unless you want every drawer in your house to be the junk drawer, make a home for household items and help them live there. In our house, Tom and I have trouble with scissors - we own 15 pairs and can never find a single one of them. We grab the Kitchen Scissors for use in a Random Closet Task, then drag out the Office Shears to perform an emergency Bathroom Cutting Need. The result? No scissors anywhere, and a lot of dull knives and sharp tempers when tags *must* be cut. The basic act of walking the barbells, boning knife or bolt cutters back to their appointed living quarters will make life easier on *you* as well as a better place for your cohabitating humans.

Time Spent: 1 minute
Calories Expended: 4
Activity Level: 2

154. Hold the Elevator

Nothing says "I am an almost decent human" like sticking your hand out to hold the elevator for that person sprinting toward the doors. It's 20 seconds of your life *including* their stop. It's also a kindness too few of us practice. Surprise everyone and give it a try. At the *very least,* stop pounding the "close door" button like it just insulted your grandmother, when you see someone heading toward your lift.

Time Spent: 20 seconds
Calories Expended: 1
Activity Level: 2

155. Pass Along a Helpful Article

My great-aunt used to clip articles from newspapers (which are still a real thing) and send them to me via snail mail. Everything from recipes to hometown news to wedding announcements, I usually got one of these from her every few weeks. I didn't always read them, but it always made me happy to know she was thinking of me. So - found a great listicle? An AI hack? Forward or otherwise share it with your peeps. This way you connect *and* provide helpful insight without paining your own brain. Even if they don't care about the information you sent - they know you care about *them*.

Time Spent: 15 seconds
Calories Expended: <1
Activity Level: 2

156. Put Your Dishes in the Dishwasher

Attention Sometime Samaritans: dishes don't crawl into the dishwasher on their own. No, really - somebody is *putting them in there*. If they're your dishes, it should be *you*. It takes no more time to put them in the machine, so avoid crusty-plate regret and stuff it in yourself. It also gives you a moment to be grateful that you *have* a dishwasher, instead of having to *be* one. Live with one of those people who has to place every spoon and plate *just so* to achieve maximum dishwasher nirvana? That's their problem.

Time Spent: 15 seconds
Calories Expended: 3
Activity Level: 2

157. Highlight a Colleague's Achievements in Public

I used to work with a woman named Cindy who never got ruffled under pressure - she once kept a class full of adult learners focused and engaged even when part of her classroom ceiling caved in! She was awesome and deserved to have people know it, so I tell this story whenever I get a chance. Sharing a short shout-out during business gatherings can make a colleague's day and take up almost none of yours.

Time Spent: 2 minutes
Calories Expended: 2
Activity Level: 3

158. Offer a Quick Tip for a Hobby

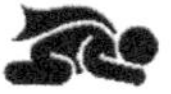

Chances are, you're way too lazy and cheap to *have* many hobbies. So, nothing on this one? No worries - move on. But if you've ever roused yourself sufficiently to make potholders or paint or stick a couple tomato plants in the ground, you can drop a casual "Try planting marigolds around your tomatoes to keep critters out of them!" when the convo turns to gardening. And who knows, you may actually get some homegrown tomatoes out of it without lifting a lazy finger!

Time Spent: 30 seconds
Calories Expended: <1
Activity Level: 2

SLAC-er Tip: Planting marigolds around your garden plot really will keep rabbits and deer from chowing down on your entire crop, but I would still plan on losing 25%. Rabbits are garden gangstas.

159. Give Precise Directions

I'm not talking a street-by-street guide to Oatmeal, Texas - they should be able to get that on Google Maps. Which, by the way, you can turn them on to if they've just crawled out of a zombie shelter or decided not to be Amish anymore or something, and still get karmic credit for this one. But what about those crowded venues where there are supposed to be hard targets like bathrooms and bars, but they're really hard to see? Instead of shrugging or pointing vaguely toward the front of the room, take 20 seconds to accurately explain where the bar is and how to get the drinks coupons. You don't want them coming back to beg a sip of *your* Shirley Temple, do you?

Time Spent: 20 seconds
Calories Expended: 3
Activity Level: 2

160. Share an Umbrella

Room for two under that golf umbrella you've got all to yourself? All your selfish instincts say "no!" But - yes, there is, so offer a couple steps worth of shelter to someone going your way. You'll be a Sometime Samaritan hero, saving their Birkin Bangs and Fairy Waves from drippy disaster, while basically just walking to your coffee place like you normally would.

Time Spent: Neutral
Calories Expended: Neutral
Activity Level: 2

161. Keep it Down at Public Events

A whispered comment to your theater buddy on how wonderful the costumes are? Okay. Otherwise, save the conversation for after the show. Because nobody bought a $15 movie ticket - much less shelled out $750 to see the Concert of the Century - to hear *your* hot takes. If someone is giving you the stink eye from the row ahead, it's because you're behaving stinkily. If your conversation is that urgent, take it outside. Because, if it's *that* urgent, what in the world are you doing at the theater anyway? Be kind to the others who are only around you because they love the things you love.

Time Spent: Neutral
Calories Expended: Negative
Activity Level: 1

162. Ask Permission to Pat That Passing Pet

Petting a stranger's dog spreads joy to the pet and its owner - a twofer! But only if pet and owner are comfortable with strangers. And of course, the penalty for not asking can be, selfishly, kinda painful. Ask if it's okay *before* you squiggle Hubert's ears, and you've set yourself up for a kind-and-considerate trifecta!

Time Spent: 30 seconds
Calories Expended: 2
Activity Level: 2

163. Help Someone Pick Up Dropped Items

Did someone overturn the okra in the produce section? Accidentally cause an apple avalanche? That's their problem. Except - *you* don't want to trip on those sprawling Sidelins, do you? Save yourself while simultaneously making the world a better place by helping the hapless shopper gather up those wayward Winesaps.

Time Spent: 15 seconds
Calories Expended: 3
Activity Level: 2

164. Fill a Birdbath

You don't have to build an aviary, whatever *that* is. But if you take one of your daily snoozes on the patio, and you already have a birdbath, it pays to drag the hose over and put water in it. The little cheepers will entertain you for free and give you something Insta-worthy to post. It will also make you look caring and outdoorsy while in reality you barely got up from your chaise lounge.

Time Spent: 2 minutes
Calories Expended: 10
Activity Level: 3

165. Stop Dropping the F-Bomb

It used to be the nuclear option of outward expression; maybe we Sometime Samaritans can make it so again? In some industries and age groups, saying the effword is not only an accepted but an *expected* part of the culture. Ok, fine. Being lazy, I don't have the energy to debate whether that's good or bad. But let's keep it confined to our personal circle of pals who think it's a wonderful word, and forebear blasting "eff" anything around children and church deacons. Since I stopped using it in general conversation, I've noticed that other people don't use it as much around me - some even *apologize* for using it. I'm selfishly self-congratulatory about de-escalating the small talk of the universe, one unuttered f-bomb at a time.

Time Spent: Negative
Calories Expended: Negative
Activity Level: 1

166. Recommend a Good Book

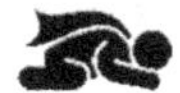

Just finished a great read? Type the title and hit "send" to a literary friend. Recommending a book you love is like giving someone a ticket to a new adventure. It's personal, thoughtful, and might just introduce them to a story or idea that changes their life. And you didn't have to write a word.

Time Spent: 15 seconds
Calories Expended: 1
Activity Level: 2

SLAC-ER Bonus: I just finished Amor Towles' *The Lincoln Highway,* which I loved, although I'm too lazy to say specifically why. Enjoy!

167. Remove Your Expired Food from the Group Fridge

That fridge isn't your personal petri dish. You put the okra casserole in there three weeks ago and you know it won't crawl out on its own - you've tried that experiment. Don't strain yourself, but do make the cool world of your communal fridge a better place by practicing a "worst in, first out" prioritization to remove your personal culinary science projects. Toss one moldy, stinky thing each day until all the gross stuff is gone, and your roommates may rethink killing you in your sleep.

Time Spent: 10 seconds
Calories Expended: <1
Activity Level: 2

168. Beaver Nuggets or Paddle Tail? Know Before You Go

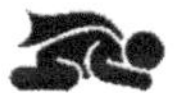

Not every quick-service restaurant has as many options as Buc-ee's, but they can be confusing if you're not a regular. Sometime Samaritans can make it easier on others who are ready to order their usual brisket kolache (which is a real thing) by figuring out what you want and *then* getting in line. Instead of standing in front of the counter or kiosk, cross-eyed and drooling, while you evaluate every option; move aside, review the food available, and get your dining plan together. Doing so costs *you* no extra time but saves others a bunch.

Time Spent: Neutral
Calories Expended: Neutral
Activity Level: 1

169. Greet With "Great to See You!"

A cheerful, "So good to see you!" is an upbeat extra to your standard SLAC-er greeting. It's an easy one to have in your back pocket because you can use it with your best friend, book-club buddy or forgotten second-grade soccer pal. Pull it out as often as your lazy self can muster up the extra energy, and improve the day of anyone who didn't just eat your last Tiny Pie.

Time Spent: 3 seconds
Calories Expended: <1
Activity Level: 2

170. Laugh at Someone's Joke

A bad dad joke. Grandma's groaner. Some people tell terrible jokes. Not off color or nasty, just bad. What's a comedic connoisseur to do? Even if it was weak, give the polite chuckle. Your friend will feel funny, in a good way. You've been supportive, in a real way, and it costs less energy than manufacturing actual wit yourself.

Time Spent: 3 seconds
Calories Expended: <1
Activity Level: 2

171. Your Meeting? Thank Them for Attending

Somehow your lazy, cheap self became the boss. And when the boss calls meetings, their team attends. Why should you thank everyone just because they sat through the meeting they were expected to show up to? Because it sets the bar for kindness and makes the world a better place with almost no effort on your part. You offer appreciation for the daily grind of showing up, which, let's be honest, you might find almost as grindy as *they* do.

Time Spent: 3 seconds
Calories Expended: <1
Activity Level: 2

172. Use Your Reusable Water Bottle

To make this suggestion fit my own rules, I *am* assuming that you already have a reusable water bottle and just aren't using it. Am I right? For the three of you who said no, skip this idea. For everyone else - get that sucker out and fill it up. Side bennie? It's a lot cheaper and easier than buying water in a one-use bottle.

Time Spent: 15 seconds
Calories Expended: 1
Activity Level: 2

SLAC-er Tip: If you like this suggestion but really don't have a reusable water bottle? Ask the next three people you see - friends, neighbors, strangers - whether they have one they'd give you. You will end up with three water bottles. Ugly ones, but still - free.

173. Gently Relocate an Insect to the Outdoors

You're going to have to deal with that skeevy scorpion one way or another. Squashing the little creepy crawler would be fast and satisfying, checking the lazy and selfish boxes for the day. But if you toss it outside, *alive,* you can feel morally superior *and* avoid the hassle of cleaning bug guts off your walls. I know - sometimes the effort is just too much for a lazy person like us. I feel you. How about this: why don't you give the errant arachnid two minutes to understand that its life hangs in the balance and, if you can't contain and release it in that time, you have my blessing to smush the little nihilist and go back to thinking about building your Roblox maze.

Time Spent: 2 minutes.
Calories Expended: 10
Activity Level: 3

174. Don't Throw Shade on Their Time in the Sun:

Skip the Snarky Comment on Their Vacation Pic

Even though we're too cheap to participate in a lot of expensive fun, we're often selfishly pissed because others *did*. Bitter because you opted out of the hiking trip or Caribbean getaway? Resist the urge to snark out "Waste of money!" under their beach pic. Even better? Turn that snarkish instinct into a karmic plus by typing "Looks amazing!" instead of leaving the world-bettering balance in neutral by just scrolling past the post.

Time Spent: 5 seconds
Calories Expended: <1
Activity Level: 2

175. Clean Out the Clothes Dryer Lint Trap

The…what? What is this "lint trap" of which you speak? Yeah, it's a real thing, and cleaning it is an incredibly easy way to make the world a better place for your family or other laundry buddies. Here's how it works: walk to your clothes dryer. Open the clothes hole. Yes, that's what I call it - stay focused. Pull out the lint trap. Pick out the fuzzy gunk that's in it. Put the lint trap back. Throw out the fuzzy gunk. Do this whenever your housemate has done your laundry yet again, and you'll have contributed not only to that task, but to actual *home maintenance.* Feel free to go strut your stuff at the hardware store.

Time Spent:
1 minute
Calories
Expended: 2
Activity Level: 2

SLAC-er Addendum: According to the National Fire Protection Association, which is a real thing, over *15,000* house fires were caused by clothes dryers in 2022. Your parakeet, roomie and neighbors will thank you for not letting yours be one of them.

176. Yes, Even If It Means Touching the Door Handle:

Trash the Hand Towel

I know - you're afraid of that germy, public bathroom door handle. Who knows what sort of vile plague lurks there? Of course you're going to wrap your hand in enough paper towels to absorb a Power Berry Big Gulp before you put one selfish finger on it. But once you have the door of doom safely ajar, don't just pitch that wad of putative paper protection in the general direction of the trash can and hope for the best. Lean back and drop it directly into the receptacle. If you have to, hold the door open with some body part while you do so. Seriously. You just used a public bathroom - you've already taken your life in your hands. Toss the towel properly; you'll survive. Probably.

Time Spent: 5 seconds
Calories Expended: <1
Activity Level: 2

177. Visualize a Positive Outcome

Let's face it – familiar with doing good we are not. Where to begin? The first step to making the world a better place is *believing* you can do it - even if you are lazy, cheap and selfish. Since seeing is believing, visualizing yourself doing good things helps you find - and act on - opportunities to do them. So instead of thinking about how bad traffic is, imagine yourself feeling great after you let someone merge at the next on-ramp. And then - *do* it!

Time Spent: 30 seconds
Calories Expended: <1
Activity Level: 2

178. Drop a "Great Point!" Into the Meeting Chat

Your colleague burnt the necessary brain cells to come up with a pertinent question or reinforcing example in the weekly status meeting? Reward that effort by throwing a "Great point!" into the chat. It's a way to engage in a meeting and be supportive of work buds without having to wake up completely.

Time Spent: 2 seconds
Calories Expended: <1
Activity Level: 2

179. Use the Sidewalk

Overgrown trees, uneven pavement, or just not being able to socialize with the giant crowd of people you're walking with can have Sometime Samaritans taking it to the streets to walk free. But studies show that pedestrians are far safer on the sidewalk than in the street. If you think about how *your* selfish self drives, this will not be surprising. And, while we can choose to walk in the road, our neighbors *can't* choose to drive on the sidewalks. Such mobility standoffs can end badly for pedestrians. And, tempting though it might be to get waited on during your recovery, it's not worth the expense of the hospital stay. Make the world a better place, and use the sidewalk when there is one.

Time Spent: Neutral
Calories Expended: Neutral
Activity Level: 1

SLAC-ER Tip: If there is no sidewalk and you must walk in the street, take that stroll on the side of the road facing into traffic (in the U.S., that's the left side). You want to see who's about to hit you, right?

180. Follow Your Friend's Business or Blog

Your friends are almost certainly way more industrious than you are. If they've started a business or launched a blog and asked you to follow their true crime or craft pickle musings - why not? It's kindness and support at the touch of a button. Down the road, you can keep racking up the karmic kindness points whenever you take 15 seconds out of watching fleece videos to like their latest post or share their new product announcement. You support your friends without buying anything. A tightwad's dream! Supportive and entrepreneur-adjacent, all from the comfort of your beanbag.

Time Spent: 15 seconds
Calories Expended: <1
Activity Level: 2

181. Help a Turtle Cross the Road Safely

If being anywhere near wildlife, let alone touching it, is not your lazy, cheap, and selfish jam, go back to your Battletoads game. But if you're willing to engage with the great outdoors, I have a suggestion. See a turtle playing Frogger on the blacktop? If the road is clear (you're not in this to get yourself killed), scoop that snapper up and move it carefully to the edge of the road in the direction it was heading. A small effort and now you're a hero to hard-shelled reptiles everywhere!

Time Spent: 2 minutes
Calories Expended: 10
Activity Level: 3

182. Refrain From the Nasty Community Reply

Every online group will have a few lunatics - don't be one of them. If someone posts something you think is silly or wrong, there's no need to call their entire gene pool into question. If you're going to spend your limited energy to respond with a correction, do so kindly. "Hi! I don't believe that's correct. According to *Made Up In Maine Gardening Facts* (which is not a real thing), papayas are not, in fact, farmed in Meddybemps. But thanks for the great fruit soup recipe!" What if they posted something impolite or unkind? Scroll on by. Online, indifference is the most powerful response. Adding to the cloud of cyber-stink is a waste of calories.

Time Spent: 10 seconds
Calories Expended: <1
Activity Level: 2

183. Nominate Great Workers for Service Awards

Did you speak to a human who solved that snarly billing problem? Have a particularly pleasant nurse during that nasty gum surgery? When service providers go above and beyond, there may be a way to recognize them beyond the thumbs-up review that still takes almost no effort on your part. QR code "say thanks" posters, end-of-call surveys - it can be really easy to give someone the public, official credit they deserve for helping lazy, selfish you. It's even possible that they'll get a bonus or some other sort of material love that you didn't have to pay for.

Time Spent: 30 seconds
Calories Expended: 1
Activity Level: 2

SLAC-ER Bonus: The Daisy Foundation helps you give official kudos to any licensed, registered nurse, nursing faculty or nursing student through their website or materials posted at healthcare providers.

184. Stop Going on the Offensive: Bury the Phrase, "No Offense, But..."

This phrase is a checkered flag for the person you are trying/not trying to offend, starting a Race to the Snarky Comeback before you've even delivered the actual insult. Every time you use it, you give away your advantage in whatever negative conversation you were about to start. Here's a thought - why not just bury the whole comment? *Not* starting a negative or belittling discussion with someone is a great way to make the world a better place. Not to mention saving yourself the energy needed to explain *why* you think their hair looks like an electrocuted hedgehog.

Time Spent: Negative
Calories Expended: Negative
Activity Level: 1

185. Go the Extra Pile:
Pick Up That *Other* Dog's Poo

You're already bending over to pick up after little Bingo - and good on you - when you notice that someone even lazier than you left *their* dog's poo to "become compost." One extra scoop into Bingo's poo-bag takes no more time or effort, so go for it. If you see that someone else has scarpered without scooping – take a few extra seconds to make the world a less publicly poopy place.

Time Spent: 15 seconds
Calories Expended: 2
Activity Level: 2

186. Mute Your Audio When You're Not Talking

Check to make sure your mic is on mute when the meeting starts. This isn't just making the meeting a better place - it's the most selfish of self-preservation tactics at work. If your sound is muted, nobody will hear you rocking out to Semisonic or snarfing your cereal when you're supposed to be absorbing that riveting new HR protocol.

Time Spent: 3 seconds
Calories: <1
Activity Level: 2

187. Don't Roll Your Eyes

Forced to listen to something completely ridiculous? When that's the case, even our lazy selves are willing to expend a calorie or two on a good eyeroll. But did you know? Rolling your eyes at someone who's sharing a sincere opinion is the universal sign for "I'm a jerk." There must be *some* reason you're listening to whatever this person is saying, so save yourself the effort and keep your eyes steady, open and pleasant.

Time Spent: Negative
Calories Expended: Negative
Activity Level: 1

SLAC-er Tip: If you absolutely *have to* roll your eyes, close them briefly and do the Internal Eye Roll. It's Secret Snark - and if they can't see it, it doesn't count.

188. Share the Sidewalk

Are you one of those selfish people who takes up the whole sidewalk with your swagger? As much as we may not want to believe it, that wee strip of mini-road wasn't built just for our one-way amble; we're supposed to share the sidewalk. Moving just one baby step to allow oncoming pedestrians to flow by - rather than forcing them into a doorway, the gutter, or the arms of a stranger - keeps us all safe and shows a critical few Sometime Samaritan seconds of kindness.

Time Spent: 5 seconds
Calories Expended: 3
Activity Level: 2

189. Appreciate a Friend for Listening

We're selfish. We know this. And usually, it means we vent our gripes and whines and then wander off to eat pineapple without so much as a "thanks" to our long-suffering pal. Just regaled your bestie with 30 minutes on your latest smoothie disappointment? Saying, "Thanks for being here to listen - I really appreciate it!" is the minimal amount of validation you can offer to justify this person's continued support.

Time Spent: 5 seconds
Calories Expended: <1
Activity Level: 2

190. Be the One-Napkin Wonder

Take Only What You Need

How many paper napkins will you actually *use*? One. Maybe two. So why do you grab a stack thick enough to insulate your attic? Contrary to our selfish assumptions, food establishments with condiment bars do not expect you to take enough salsa, sweetener and stir sticks to stock your zombie apocalypse shelter. So, take what you need, and make the world a better place by leaving some for the next person.

Time Spent: Negative
Calories Expended: Negative
Activity Level: 1

191. Make a Media Connection

Do you Love Lucy? Or are you into Only Murders in the Building? Whatever says This Is Us to you, bring others into your world by sharing your TV/streaming faves new and old. Whether it's gene pool, geography, or genre, you can create a connection with friends and family by sharing episodes and clips from your personal five-star list. All this interaction, without having to think up your own original content!

Time Spent: 30 seconds
Calories Expended: <1
Activity Level: 2

SLAC-er Bonus: Tom recommends season 9, episode 21: "The Case of the Twice-Told Twist" to courtroom-classic *Perry Mason* fans.

192. Hop In! I'll Slow Down a Little
Give Someone a Ride to an Event

Why not get credit for doing something nice when you're already doing it anyway? If it's on your way, offer your bestie a ride to that spin class you're driving over to watch, er, participate in. Pull up to the curb and let them hop in. You get karmic credit for a personal *and* environmental kindness, with extra points if you come to a full and complete stop.

Time Spent: 1 minute
Calories Expended: 3
Activity Level: 2

193. Suggest a Local Park for Relaxation

I know. Selfishly, the last thing you want to do is encourage other people to show up at your favorite outdoor napping spot. But really? It's a big park, and you don't have to share where *you* normally hang out. Just put it out there: "Ever been to Muddy Mitten Park? It's a hidden gem." Sharing the deets on a local patch of happiness increases both theirs and yours.

Time Spent: 5 seconds
Calories Expended: <1
Activity Level: 2

194. It's No LOL Matter: Don't Text in Class

You may doubt this, but I've tried it a couple times and it's true: you *can survive* 45 minutes without otter videos and poo emojis. As a matter of fact, IRL is having a moment, and experiencing it while getting an education is a SLAC-er twofer. So really - eyes up, phone down. The last thing you need is a video of the instructor berating you in front of the whole class to go viral.

Time Spent: Neutral
Calories Expended: Negative
Activity Level: 1

195. Donate Food You Won't Eat to a Food Bank

Volunteering your weekends at a food bank? Yeah, no. Not going to happen. But you *can* help the hungry without breaking a sweat. That unopened jar of pickled whatsis you'll never touch? Perfect for a food bank. As long as it's unexpired, unopened and untainted, it helps someone else. Bonus? Your pantry gets cleaned out, one can of creamed corn at a time.

Time Spent: 2 minutes
Calories Expended: 10
Activity Level: 3

SLAC-er Tip: BOLO for Boy Scout "Scouting for Food" drives and office charity collection containers. They often appear around the year-end holidays. Waiting for these oh-so-easy opportunities to give ensures that you don't strain yourself trying to find a centralized donation point.

196. Mind the Meeting

People like us - the ones talking to pals instead of taking part in the meeting - are one reason there are so many *follow-up* meetings. Still having those sidebar conversations at the stand-up? And you're *surprised* you didn't get that promotion? If you've got a question, everyone will benefit from hearing it. Just snarking? Wait for lunch.

Time Spent: Neutral
Calories Expended: Negative
Activity Level: 1

197. Tell a Joke

This can be a minefield for Sometime Samaritans who don't always think through what we're about to say. Here's a tip: you almost can't go wrong with a self-deprecating joke. More good news? You don't have to pull a mental muscle thinking of a good one - AI can do the work. I just asked ChatGPT to "Please write me an inoffensive, self-deprecating joke." Here's what I got: "I'm so bad at multitasking, I got distracted making toast this morning and replied to my boss *'Is it crispy enough?'* when they thanked me for getting my status report in on time." It's not going to get you a guest spot on *Smartless*, but everyone will get a little chuckle and walk away smiling.

Time Spent: 15 seconds
Calories Expended: 1
Activity Level: 2

SLAC-er Addendum: Saying "please" when I ask ChatGPT to do something isn't getting me any karmic kindness points, but it *is* good practice.

198. Acknowledge That They're Upset

You're with a friend. A really, really upset (but not with *you*) friend. Every lazy, selfish bone in your body is whispering "Slouch away. Let someone else deal with it." But you have to try to help, so you can both get to that trivia meetup. How about: put a hand on their arm and calmly say, "I'm here for you. Vent a little." A hug might even be in order. It's disarmingly simple, even kind of zen-master-y. And remember - this is a *friend*. You're going to want this person around for *you* someday. So, commit two whole minutes to talking them off the ledge. Unless they're literally, you know, *on a ledge*. Then go get real help, however much it messes up your game night.

Time Spent: 2 minutes
Calories Expended: 3
Activity Level: 3

199. Take a Load Off – Them: Offer to Carry Something

You have my permission to strategically avoid those lunatics who are lugging boxes the size of a Mini Cooper into the local UPS, but – if you're going the same direction and you have a free hand? Offer to grab a package or help out with that 5th bag of groceries. Helping someone juggle that item into the P.O. makes the world a better place. It also reduces the likelihood that you'll have to stop when they drop whatever it is in front of your car when you're trying to get home for your nap.

Time Spent: 2 minutes
Calories Expended: 5
Activity Level: 3

200. Report Spam or Harmful Content

All the garbage that needs to be cleaned up isn't lying on the street. But just like out in the physical world, cyber junk piles up when SLAC-ers don't pitch in to get rid of it. Nobody expects you to follow through constantly, reporting every suspiciously charming puppy rescuer who's just dying to friend you, but. You can help others by blowing a quarter-calorie on diligence every once in awhile. See something online that's nasty, harmful or otherwise making the world a less-nice place? Click "Report." Select "Spam." Done. This easy action makes the internet a little safer, thanks to digital citizen superhero you.

Time Spent: 10 seconds
Calories Expended: <1
Activity Level: 2

201. Share a Feel-Good Story

Did you happen to see a heart-warming story in the news? Pass it along. Deliver the deets on the 104-year-old skydiver or the dog who rescued a toddler through the social media outlet of your choice. Sharing happy news is an exponential world-improver, even with *your* limited friend base. It gives everyone a break from doom-scrolling and negativity, with the added bonus of making you look like someone who keeps up with what's going on in the world. Double added bonus: it will make *you* happier, too.

Time Spent: 2 minutes
Calories Expended: 3
Activity Level: 2

SLAC-er Bonus: *Today Online* keeps a running list of this type of happy story. Check them out to keep your own mind turned toward the sunny side of life while finding friendly fodder to share with others.

202. I Might Need Your ChapStick, Too: No Talking in Class

Sometimes we selfish grownups forget the basic lessons learned in kindergarten and treat educational opportunities as social time. That's a bit of a laff riot, since we never voluntarily interact with other humans when we're *not* in class. So we know this, but I'm going to remind everyone. Talking over the instructor in any type of class? Even dopey ones? Not cool. I mean, there may actually be people in the class who *want to learn*. You may not be one of them, but somebody paid for this course, and I'm assuming they expect you to get some benefit out of it. If you need to borrow a charger or bum a tater tot, do it quickly and with a minimum of discussion. Otherwise stay quiet, look respectful, and bonus: you'll avoid missing something that might actually help you pass that certification exam.

Time Spent: Neutral
Calories Expended: Negative
Activity Level: 1

203. Compliment the Host's Cooking

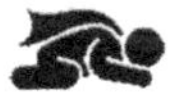

You didn't have to buy it. You didn't have to *cook* it. You didn't even have to set the table. Someone is hosting you for a meal. So even if it wasn't your absolute favorite - make a little fuss. "This kale is so flavorful!" or, "You really nailed the texture of this okra." The kindly simple, "Thank you for the lovely meal" is a good catch-all for the superlatively lazy among us. Your minimal appreciation for food that didn't arrive in a bag could even get you invited back again.

Time Spent: 10 seconds
Calories Expended: <1
Activity Level: 2

204. Take Three Deep Breaths to Calm Yourself

If you're stressed out, you're likely to do something that changes the world, all right - but not in a *good* way. You can avoid that outcome, however, and you don't need to pay a therapist or even, heaven forbid, exercise, to do it. To let off steam instead of blowing up, close your eyes and inhale slowly. Exhale slowly. Repeat. Repeat again. It resets your brain like a mini power nap, but without the awkward drooling, and gives you a chance to rethink that tirade you were about to unleash. Bonus? The target of the averted snarkpocalypse probably walked away while you chillaxed.

Time Spent: 30 seconds
Calories Expended: <1
Activity Level: 2

205. SLAC-ers Can Save Lives Without Lifting a Finger

Be an Organ Donor

Did you know that, at any given time in the U.S., there are *100,000* people waiting for transplants? This is an easy one. Answer a few questions on a website so, when you croak, you *save someone's life*. Probably more than one. If you choose to be an organ donor, you help people who desperately need a heart, kidney, lung or liver. Yeah, okay - maybe nobody should have your liver. But still. There are several easy ways to sign up, including ticking the "organ donor" box when you get or renew your driver's license. One box-tick. I can't think of anything we lazy, cheap and selfish people could do that would have more impact with less effort.

Time Spent: 2 minutes
Calories Expended: 3
Activity Level: 3

SLAC-er Addendum: Are you ready to make this commitment? Yay you! Sign up by state at organdonor.gov/sign-up.

206. Use Your Cheapskate Superpower: Tell Friends About the Free Museum Day

As proud penny-pinchers, we gather information about freebies. And nothing gets our lazy behinds up off the couch like a free whatever! Make it a group win by kindly sharing with your buds. "First Saturdays at the art museum are free!" is all it takes and, *voilà*! You've done something kind and culture-y without spending a dime of your own money. And you've spoken French.

Time Spent: 30 seconds
Calories Expended: <1
Activity Level: 2

207. Proliferate Your Playlist

Music loving SLAC-ers, I'm talking to *you*. Just finished building that killer throwback playlist? A compendium of your favorite kazoo instrumentals? Since you already built it for yourself - let your Bach-loving besties know it's there. Maybe even give strangers access to it. Share those happy sounds before it's over, oops, out of time.

Time Spent: 15 seconds
Calories Expended: 1
Activity Level: 2

208. Admire a DIY Project

How did you get such talented friends? They build furniture. They tile bathrooms. They landscape their yards instead of just watering the weeds. It's true - some people are vastly less lazy and selfish than we are. They have the talent and gumption to do all sorts of amazing home projects. Know somebody like this? Take the opportunity to keep these active, handy people motivated and feeling good. "I'm so impressed that you tiled the whole bathroom, instead of just the parts you can see from the living room!" That's all it takes. They feel proud and, if you play your cards right, maybe you can get them to come over and fix your sink.

Time Spent: 10 seconds
Calories Expended: <1
Activity Level: 2

209. Let Someone in on Your Best Tech Hack

Hey tech weenie: you have a killer timesaving or otherwise super-cool app hack, and it's easy enough to explain in less than two minutes. Good for you! Now, share it with your struggling colleague or Wordle pal. You'll be helpful while reinforcing your genius and minimizing your actual brain strain. The best hack I ever *shared*? Use a social-media scheduler app to automate your social posts. The best one I ever *received*? That you can schedule an email to auto-send at a crazy hour when you're not actually working. Like naptime.

Time Spent: 2 minutes.
Calories Expended: <1
Activity Level: 2

210. Do a Quick Breakroom Tidy

Do you know how much coffee sludge you can get off a countertop in two minutes? A lot. Even if you do it really, really slowly. So take two minutes or less to languidly make the breakroom or some other public area at work a better place. Straighten a few chairs. Wipe off a counter or a shelf in the common fridge. Don't touch anything truly gross - a slime-altering altruist you are not - but you can stand the skwickies of scooping up some mystery crumbs with a paper towel once in a blue moon.

Time Spent: 2 minutes
Calories Expended: 10
Activity Level: 3

211. Flip the Switch, Save the Planet

Turning off one light when you leave the room might sound like the kind of advice that only your smug enviro-pal would give. But hold your eye roll - this microscopic action actually packs a pretty impressive punch. Let's say every American turned off *just one* 60-watt light bulb for an hour every day. That's enough energy to power a 55-inch LED TV for more than *220 million hours!* The impact? Every single person in the U.S. could watch their six favorite seasons of *My Lottery Dream Home...* twice. Whoa. Are you already saving energy with LED bulbs? Good on you! But turning them off for the same amount of time *still* delivers 37 million hours of binge-watching. Which would let every American stream every episode of *Mystery Science Theater 3000*. Oh, the humanity!

Time Spent: 1 second
Calories Expended: <1
Activity Level: 2

212. Be Careful Where You Throw Your Butt

Tossing cigarette butts on the ground makes you Smokey the Bear's #1 PSA poster child. Crush it, douse it, bin it, and avoid becoming an amateur arsonist. Also stop smoking. It's expensive and it could kill you. Just sayin.

Time Spent:30 seconds
Calories Expended: 3
Activity Level: 2

SLAC-er Addendum: The U.S. Fire Administration, which is a real thing, estimates that there were 7,800 fires, 275 deaths, 750 injuries and over $36M in financial loss in 2021 due to smoking in residences. This doesn't even include open-air, butt-related conflagrations.

213. Encourage a Colleague Who Seems Stressed

Everyone has bad days at work, but it's surprising how much a minimal show of support can help. This is a great chance to do good while doing almost nothing! A quick, "Hey, this too shall pass, hang in there," can be incredibly reassuring, and you can say it on your way to the restroom so they can't completely break down and take up too much of your time.

Time Spent: 15 seconds
Calories Expended: <1
Activity Level: 2

214. Wipe the Mirror

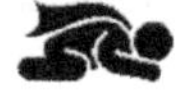

Nobody wants to look through that film of hairspray you overshot onto the mirror. Or, for that matter, any other goo, glop, or gelatinous mess you could possibly fling onto a reflective surface while getting ready to watch TV. A quick wipe now saves Sometime Samaritans the hassle of getting out the ice pick and hazmat suit needed for the really big clean. That said, I estimated the time and calories for this one based on your lazy self only cleaning that mirror when you can't recognize your own face in it. Still worth it.

Time Spent: 2 minutes
Calories Expended: 6
Activity Level: 3

215. Dust - Sporadically

The thought of dusting a whole house or even an office cubicle that will just get dusty again in a few days makes most of us chuckle lazily and roll over for another 15 minutes of shuteye. What's the *point*? The point is: a clean world is a happy world. Not enough? It will also reduce the amount of sneezing others do in your general vicinity, and keep you healthier too. Check out the SLAC-er Tip below - this one's easier than you think.

Time Spent: 2 Minutes
Calories Expended: 10
Activity Level: 3

SLAC-er Tip: Carry a Swiffer, rag or feather duster around with you for an hour one day each week, and wipe whatever you pass on your way to wherever you're going anyway. Don't stop - don't even slow down - just...wipe. You will be amazed.

216. Don't Stuff Your Coat into the Overhead Bin

Seriously - the luggage rules have been the same since airplanes had smoking sections - one item in the overhead bin, everything else you schlepped with you mashed into the corners of your personal seating space. Same for trains, buses and any other conveyance that has limited shared space for passengers' stuff. Lazy, cheap, and selfish we may be, but we're not stupid; we know the rules, so let's obey them. Hang on to that giant puffer coat you think you're going to need in Atlanta. If, and only *if*, all other bags are stowed, and you see a cranny where your beauty of a barn jacket can fit, go for it. Otherwise? Snuggle under all that fabulous faux fur and take your regularly scheduled nap.

Time Spent: Neutral
Calories Expended: Neutral
Activity Level: 1

217. Print on Both Sides of the Paper

Hey cheapos - I'm talking to *you*! I've got a great suggestion to cut what you pay for printer paper in exactly half. Just set your "Print" defaults to print on *both* sides of the paper, instead of just one. Many apps default to this setting, which means all you have to do to make the world a more tree-filled place is - nothing. And really, what are you saving the other side of that paper *for*?

Time Spent: 20 seconds
Calories Expended: <1
Activity Level: 2

SLAC-er Tip: Did a few one-page prints slip through? Don't go to pieces! Remember, you can use the clean side as scrap for notes and grocery lists.

218. Sneeze into Your Elbow, Head Angled Downward

When sneezing, most people don't lift their chin and let fly like they're Maria in *The Sound of Music*, but still. Muffling a sneeze with your hand is you *trying* to be considerate - until you pass someone a pickle with that moist, germy mitt. You've seen the posters, SLACers, now live the dream - sneeze into the crook of your elbow, while tilting your head down and away from others, and you might single-handedly ensure that we're not all stuck in our houses for a year. Again.

Time Spent: Neutral
Calories Expended: Neutral
Activity Level: 1

219. Write that Angry Epistle - Then Delete It

Every once in a while, someone you know is going to say something truly stupid - even downright mean. At work, it will probably happen five times before lunch. And on social media? Fuhgeddaboudit. In our anonymous, digital world, it's so easy to bite back. To write the scathing retort and hit "Post" before you think it through.

But ask yourself; what will any of us get out of you blasting that blowback? Will you come off as wise and strong? Will the subject of your vitriol change their evil ways? Will the witnesses to this nasty little drama be influenced to do good going forward? If not, why don't you just peel another pineapple and watch a few cat videos?

If it helps you blow off a little steam, go ahead and write the nasty note. Then take a few cleansing breaths. Then delete it. From the screen *and* from your memory. Life is too short and we're way too selfish to waste time sustaining pointless drama.

Time Spent: 2 minutes
Calories Expended: 3
Activity Level: 2

220. Give Gossip a Hard Pass

Are there really so many people still willing to be friends with you that you can afford to humiliate them with willy-nilly willful snark? One of the best things we can *stop* doing as Sometime Samaritans is spreading gossip. Gossip makes the world a worse place for the people you like most. What a waste of friendship, and what a waste of effort! All that scheming and whispering, and the result is a rancid cloud of negativity we don't even get paid to create? Feh. So, just once, when someone messages you that mess - ignore it. Let it die with you. Extend your naptime and make the world a better place while you do it.

Time Spent: Negative
Calories Expended: Negative
Activity Level: 1

221. Power Down = Power Up

Turn Your Game Console All the Way Off

Hey, Legend. You know that feeling when you clear a dungeon and unlock a bonus chest full of loot you barely had to fight for? That's what it's like to fully shut down your game console when you're not using it. Because here's the thing: your Xbox or PlayStation in "rest mode" is basically a background NPC, draining extra power from your energy bill - and the planet. If you wouldn't leave your controller vibrating on the couch overnight, don't let your system suck down energy while you sleep. Be the hero the grid deserves. No side quest required.

Time Spent: 10 seconds
Calories Expended: 2
Activity Level: 2

222. Offer a High Five

Is it time to express somewhat exuberant congrats? Expend five seconds of energy on a high five. The happiest of handshake alternatives, the high five is a great way to amp up the positivity without any more effort than raising your hand above your shoulder. True - too much of a high-fiving good thing and you get into David Puddy territory, but I'm counting on your innate inertia to help you avoid that.

Time Spent: 5 seconds
Calories Expended: 3
Activity Level: 2

SLAC-er Addendum: In the spirit of giving credit where credit is due (and racking up my word-bettering points for the day) - thank you to my wonderful neighbor Sara for thinking of this one. High five, girlfriend!

223. Forgive a Friend for a Small Mistake

They forgot your dog's birthday or canceled your burger night at the last minute. Not cool. But is this normally a good person? A good friend? Then let it go. You save emotional energy and get to take the moral high ground without even climbing. And let's be real - you *know* you'll be the offender at some point - being understanding this time may help the situation when it's *your* apology being offered.

Time Spent: Negative
Calories Expended: Negative
Activity Level: 1

224. Tuck it In, Flip it Over, Point it Out

Sometime Samaritans are rarely arbiters of style. But we *do* want our buddies to look their best, even if *our* wear-to-the-store "fancy" bathrobe has seen better days. Gently pointing out a twisted collar or visible t-shirt tag - or the classic nightmare of TP on the shoe - is a thoughtful thing to do. And you may even consider leaning over to fix it, assuming you know this person well enough to invade their space. It's a lazy little demonstration that you have your buddy's back - literally.

Time Spent: 5 seconds
Calories Expended: 1
Activity Level: 2

225. Get Going at That Green Light

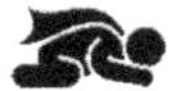

Having to stop for a red traffic light drives everyone crazy. But when it happens, a lot of us drop into a mysterious fugue state or mindless phone-scrolling. This can lead to us being single-handedly responsible for the 10 cars behind us having to sit through the same traffic light *again*. Ouch. Causing 75 seconds of frustration for up to 40 people is *not* making the world a better place. Keep an eye on the light and go - safely - when it turns green. Yes, this could mean missing out on a riveting puppy video or saving the rest of that P.Terry's double until you get home. A small sacrifice for a big impact.

Time Spent: Negative
Calories Expended: Neutral
Activity Level: 1

226. Shut Off the Water When Brushing Your Teeth

A couple quick turns of the tap and you've made the world a better place before breakfast! Turning off the water while you stare into space brushing your teeth is one of the brainiest no-brainer ways you can stay lazy, cheap, and selfish and still change the world. The average faucet spits out 2.2 gallons of water per minute - that's 4.4 gallons wasted every time you run through your dental routine. That's enough water to make 35 venti iced coffees, wash a small load of laundry, or hydrate a camel through a light cardio session. If every American did this just once a day, we'd save over one *billion* gallons of water - *every week.*

Time Spent: 5 seconds
Calories Expended: <1
Activity Level: 2

SLAC-er Addendum: The camel example is almost certainly *not* a real thing.

227. Put One Toilet Seat . . .UP

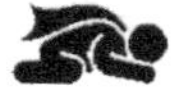

I know. It's not proper etiquette. It doesn't look nice. And we ladies have been trying for *decades* to train our guys to put that seat *down*. But if you're lucky enough to have two bathrooms, why not make one "his?" It costs us nothing in time or effort, and it may be the best gift we've ever given him - without spending a dime. It also gives *him* the opportunity to make the world a better place by cleaning "his" commode. We may be changing the world, but we still have our lazy, selfish agenda.

Time Spent: 10 seconds
Calories Expended: 3
Activity Level: 2

228. Compare Childhood Memories

Pop a couple 'Member Berries and bring out a back-in-the-day memory to share with the group. *"Remember Slip 'n Slides?" "Remember Polly Pockets?"* This is one of my favorite go-to's when we're on hour two of toe-fungus stories or someone's about to Go Political. Yeah, it will date you - but you'll get a light, fun conversation going, every time.

Time Spent: 30 seconds
Calories Expended: <1
Activity Level: 2

SLAC-er Bonus: Remember "Weebles wobble but they don't fall down."? I 'member!

229. Tell Someone They Have a Great Laugh

It's amazing how pushing out a few syllables of positivity can make the world a better place. "You have the best laugh." That's it. Doesn't cost a dime, it makes them feel like a ray of sunshine, and they'll probably laugh again just because you said it. Which is a win for you both.

Time Spent: 5 seconds
Calories Expended: <1
Activity Level: 2

230. Don't Hog the Armrest

In almost every public venue where armrests are present, there will be 1.5 armrests for every 2 arms that want them. What's a lazy, cheap and selfish person to do? Answer - share. The alternative is bruised elbows and jangled nerves as you fight two *other* selfish people for control of both. Now that you've committed to doing this particular good deed, which one should you struggle for? Fret not, SLAC-er: there is actually a *rule* for armrest allocation. In a long row of seats, like in a theater, you get the armrest to your right. This includes the right-hand cup holder too, if you're lucky enough to have *that* dilemma. I have no idea who gets however many armrests are left over, but you can puzzle that out on a day where you're not trying to make the world a better place.

Time Spent: Neutral
Calories Expended: Neutral
Activity Level: 1

SLAC-er Bonus: Did cheapo you book the middle seat on an airplane? In this case, frugality is its own reward because - you get *both* armrests!

231. Like Water for Weimaraners

Set Out Water for Neighbors' Pets

Love to watch the neighbors and their sweet dogs walk by while dozing on your porch swing? Those neighbors - and their fur babies - might appreciate a bowl of water placed at the end of your driveway, so Bingo can keep hydrated during his promenade. It costs nothing (assuming you have a spare bowl), takes almost no effort, and gets you back on the porch before you have to talk to anyone.

Time Spent: 2 minutes
Calories Expended: 5
Activity Level: 3

232. Acknowledge Service Providers When Others Don't

Was the customer in front of you channeling the *Father of the Bride* matrimonial meltdown of George Banks with their unlucky service provider? You have the power to pump them up while barely exerting yourself. No need to jump into the fray - you're too selfish to spend the night in the hoosgow. But, when it's your turn to interact with that cashier, a quick "You were really patient with that last customer" might put their day back on a sunny track.

Time Spent: 15 seconds
Calories Expended: <1
Activity Level: 2

233. Applaud

For those of you who are ambitious enough to try a little exercise, I've got a great world-improver for you: clapping. Clapping takes zero thought, looks like quite a bit of effort, and is both enthusiastic and supportive without the need for you to think up detailed praise. So, make some happy noise! It will completely justify that nap you already planned to take.

Time Spent: 10 seconds
Calories Expended: 6
Activity Level: 3

SLAC-er Bonus: Want to applaud in sign language? Hold up both of your hands at head level, palm out, and waggle them in what we often call "jazz hands" form.

234. Make a Habit of It

Are you ready to go Next-Level World-Improver? Choose any *one* of these suggestions and do it as often as you can. Stop at *every* red light. *Always* put those scissors back where they belong. *Don't* say the nasty thing. *Do* say the *nice* thing. Tidy up, reuse or reach out whenever the opportunity presents itself.

If you do that one nice thing over and over until you no longer have to think about it, that's a *habit,* friends and neighbors. One you can be proud of.

And That's It

Congratulations! Yay you! Thank you for doing a world of good. With as little effort as possible.

Even if you completed exactly one of these suggestions, one time last March, you've made the world a better place. It's true: you didn't cure cancer. You didn't teach someone to read. You didn't even figure out how to get rid of that scaly gunk in the shower. But - you helped. You improved. You made the world a teeny, tiny bit better than it was. Your SLAC-er self did good, and you are officially a Sometime Samaritan.

So take a moment to bask in your general fabulousness. What the heck - take two. Then get out there and do just a little bit more.

XO - Diane

Join The Sometime Samaritans

Whoa - I'm exhausted. It's definitely naptime. But when we're both ready to continue this conversation, come see us! We're here:

Follow The Sometime Samaritans Facebook Page where you can lurk and laugh without lifting a finger.

Join the Sometime Samaritans Group on Facebook to post your own lazy, cheap, and selfish selfies.

You can also follow us on Instagram. Whatever.

Looking for a lazy, cheap, and selfish speaker for your library, club, church or corporate event? I don't work during naptime, but let's talk when I'm awake. Email me: sometimesamaritans@gmail.com.

Acknowledgements

It's out of character, but I'm going to muster up the energy to thank those folks who've been in my corner while I created this book. It really is the least I can do. But first - let's get my personal Acknowledgement of Ineptitude out of the way.

Remember - I'm lazy. Any typos, incorrect references or other slothful slipups are completely my fault. None of the products or businesses referenced in this work have endorsed me, the book or, to my knowledge, anyone I've ever met. That said - many of said products and businesses are big faves of mine; some of them I just used in the book because they sound kind of funny.

Now the good stuff. A huge shoutout and sooooo many thanks to my initial core of confidants, cheerleaders, and contributors: Kathy Almonte, Susan Bobus, Sara Bromley, Kirsten Butzow, Joanna Callaway, Jenny Duckworth, Melissa Fong, Kim Foster, Pauline Guest, Ruth Hogan, Gloria Hughes, Rebecca Kalogeris, Karen Leffler, Ann Mason, Leslie Mayher, Pat McDermott, Lisa Moore, Dave Oakley, Carol Pickering, Betsy Pierson, Colleen Pierson, Karla Walter, Jodi Ziegert, Mark Ziegert, and Sharon Znilek. I appreciate you being there to like the early social posts, give me editorial input, ask me how it's going and in general aid and abet the fun I've been having. You are all 100% Samaritans in addition to being amazing humans; I'm lucky to know you.

Gratitude to my fabulous stepdaughter and acknowledged Shopping Cart Vigilante Hillary Carrigan for her encouragement and group posts – she's making the world a better place, one shopping cart at a time.

Thanks to my dad Jerry Harbaugh for watching videos of me shutting blinds and picking up garbage, and looking at endless versions of Dee, Essy and Tommy, all rendered badly, without once rolling his eyes. You and mom taught me how to be a Samaritan - although I flatter myself that the lazy, cheap, and selfish bits are all me.

And of course, thanks, applause, love and high fives to my editor, husband and BFF, Tom Pierson. It's fun because you're doing it with me - I heart you bigtime.

About the Author

Diane grew up in Michigan. She worked as a market strategist and product leader for tech companies on the East Coast, later speaking and advising on best practices in those disciplines around the world. She's the author of the strategic innovation playbook, *How to Innovate on Purpose*.

Currently, Diane lives in Austin with her husband Tom and their exceptionally lazy, cheap, and selfish Siamese cat. She enjoys napping and buying slippers.

Sometime
Samaritans

Made in the USA
Coppell, TX
07 February 2026

71399892R00148